Brandon

The football is signed by Bobby & Terry Bowen — who this book is about

Love
Pop-pop Hassan
&
Grandma Marie
9/01

WINNING'S
ONLY PART
OF THE GAME

WINNING'S ONLY PART OF THE GAME

OF THE GAME

Lessons of Life & Football

BOBBY, TERRY & THE BOWDEN FAMILY

WITH **BEN BROWN**

WARNER BOOKS

A Time Warner Company

Warner Books, Inc., 1271 Avenue of the Americas, New York, NY 10020

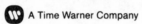 A Time Warner Company

Printed in the United States of America
First Printing: September 1996
10 9 8 7 6 5 4 3 2 1

Library of Congress Cataloging-in-Publication Data

Bowden, Bobby.
    Winning's only part of the game : lessons of life and football /
  Bobby Bowden and family with Ben Brown.
        p.   cm.
    ISBN 0-446-52050-0
    1. Bowden, Bobby. 2. Football coaches—Florida—Biography.
  3. Football coaches—Florida—Family relationship. I. Brown, Ben,
  1946–   . II. Title.
  GV939.B66A34   1996
  796.332'092—dc20
  [B]   96-5540
                                                              CIP

Book design and composition by L & G McRee

To the memory of those who came before:
Bob Pierce Bowden, Sunset Bowden, Althea Estock, and George Estock.
And to all the Bowdens who will come after.

ACKNOWLEDGMENTS

Winning's Only Part of the Game grew out of an idea by Warner Books editor Rick Wolff, who, in the spring of 1995, talked to my literary agent, Joel Fishman, about a book of Bowden family correspondence. When we began work, a more natural form evolved: dialogue, written as if members of the family were in the same room.

Once we hit on that style, it was easy to shape conversations around topics we thought would interest readers—especially readers who are drawn more to the give-and-take of family relationships and to the lessons that can be learned from high-pressure competition than to the X's and O's of football strategy.

All the conversations were created especially for this book and edited from some fifty hours of in-person interviews and telephone discussions that took place between July and December of 1995.

We owe special thanks to the Bowden spouses and children, who surrendered precious chunks of family time so we could talk at all hours of the day and night; to Christine Gardinier, my wife, for her indulgence; and to the traffic managers and resource providers in the two universities' athletic departments—Sue Hall, Mark Meleney, and Rob Wilson at Florida State; and Jean Davis, Kent Partridge, and Scott Stricklin at Auburn.

BEN BROWN

CONTENTS

Part II · LESSONS OF THE GAME 103

THE BOWDENS

BOBBY BOWDEN   Born 1929 in Birmingham, Alabama, Bobby attended one semester at the University of Alabama in Tuscaloosa. He transferred to what was then Howard College in Birmingham (later called Samford University), where he was Little All-America in football.

After head coaching jobs at two small schools, including his alma mater, Bobby became an assistant at Florida State University in 1963, then an assistant at West Virginia, before rising to head coach at West Virginia in 1970.

He took over a struggling FSU program in 1976 and hasn't had a losing season since that first year. Going into the 1996 season, his twenty-first at FSU, Bowden's career record was 259-81-4. His teams had not lost a bowl game since 1980, and since 1986 had not finished a season ranked lower than No. 4 in the country.

In 1993, the Seminoles under Bowden won their first national championship.

Among active coaches, only Penn State's Joe Paterno has more career wins. The only I-A coaches ahead of Paterno and Bowden on the all-time win list are legends Bear Bryant, Pop Warner, and Amos Alonzo Stagg.

Bobby and his wife, Ann, have six children, plus twenty-one grandchildren.

JULIA ANN ESTOCK BOWDEN Ann was born in Gadsden, Alabama, in 1932 and moved with her family to Birmingham when she was in her teens. High school sweethearts, she and Bobby married when she was sixteen.

Ann attended Howard College with Bobby, but quit before getting a degree in order to devote all her energy to raising their growing family. She still travels with Bobby on their annual month-long tour of booster clubs each spring. She serves on the board of the Florida Baptist Children's Home, but her primary role in the family now is doting grandmother.

ROBYN BOWDEN HINES The Bowden's oldest child was born in 1951 in Birmingham. She married her high school boyfriend, Jack Hines, who played football at West Virginia under her father.

She's a teacher in Auburn, where Hines coaches on the defensive staff for her brother Terry. They have two children.

STEVE BOWDEN Born 1952 in Birmingham, Steve played for his dad at West Virginia. He became an ordained minister with a Ph.D. in philosophy, taught college, and served as a higher education administrator. He has five children and resides in the Birmingham area.

TOMMY BOWDEN Tommy, who was born in Birmingham in 1954, also played for his father at West Virginia. He was on the fast track as an assistant coach at Duke, Alabama, and Kentucky until he walked into a rat's nest at Auburn in 1991, the year he took the job of offensive coordinator under Pat Dye. The school was under investigation by the National Collegiate Athletic Association; the team suffered through two break-even seasons; and Dye was forced to resign.

He lost his coordinator title in 1993, when his younger brother Terry took over the program. He regained his title in 1994 and is credited with helping his brother develop one of the most potent and balanced offenses in Auburn history.

Tommy is expected to become the next Bowden head football coach within the next two or three seasons. He's the father of two.

TERRY BOWDEN Born in Douglas, Georgia, in 1956, Terry played running back at West Virginia and graduated with a 3.65 grade point average in accounting. He got his law degree from Florida State while serving as a graduate assistant in football under his dad.

At twenty-six, he was the youngest head coach in America when he took over the Salem College (West Virginia) program in 1983. In his second year, he led the school to its second conference championship in eighty years. He won eighteen of his last twenty-four games there.

Terry became head coach at Samford, his parents' alma mater, in 1987. His team went 9–1 that first year, and he led the Division III program to Division I-AA rankings, where Samford was competing for national championship honors by 1991.

In 1993, he took over a troubled Auburn program just as the school was placed on two years probation. His first season team went undefeated. His second finished 9-1-1 in 1994. Both teams were prevented by the conditions of Auburn's probation from going on to bowl games. His 1995 Tigers (8–3) went to their first bowl game since 1990.

When he took over at Auburn, Terry and his dad became the first father-son combo to be coaching different teams in the top tier of college football at the same time. Terry has five daughters.

JEFF BOWDEN   The youngest son was born in Birmingham in 1959 and played for his father at Florida State. He coached with Terry at Salem and Samford, then spent three years as receivers coach at Southern Mississippi, where he played Tommy's Auburn team.

Jeff joined his father at Florida State in 1994 to coach wide receivers. He has four children.

GINGER BOWDEN MADDEN   Born 1961 in Birmingham, the Bowdens' youngest grew up in Tallahassee and married John Madden, who played football for Bobby at Florida State.

After having two children, Ginger returned to Florida State and then went on to law school. She graduated in 1994 and works as a prosecutor in Fort Walton Beach, Florida.

She gave birth to her third son in September of 1995.

WINNING'S ONLY PART OF THE GAME

INTRODUCTION

By Ann Bowden

Every year, I can count on getting calls from reporters, usually from a paper or a magazine a long way from Tallahassee, who want to know about "the real Bobby Bowden." What they suspect, I guess, is that there's some secret other Bobby, separate from the one they see in interviews or on the sidelines on Saturday.

Well, there probably is, since we all have secret parts we don't let others see. Not even the people closest to us. But if there's a Bobby Bowden that differs a whole lot from the image most people have of him—except, perhaps, for one important thing I'll get to in a minute—he's kept it hidden from me.

Over the years, I think Bobby has learned that people especially take to certain parts of his personality—his love of a good story, for instance, or his willingness to make himself (or me) the butt of a joke. So he's built on that. He has taken the Bobby Bowden he started with and added more of the same ingredients to become the Coach Bowden everybody knows.

Here's the key ingredient: All his life Bobby has had the ability to make people feel at ease when they're with him, and he's consciously developed that. People he's met all over the world are convinced they're among his closest friends. It's a gift he has. It's one of the things that attracted me to him when we were teens in Birmingham five decades ago. And it's served him well as a coach and as a Christian leader.

Bobby's Christian commitment is the genuine article. While he won't use his position to preach at people who aren't interested or to impose his personal beliefs, there's no doubt where he stands. He believes in the same God he learned about in his parents' home and in Sunday school as a child. He accepts the Bible as the Word of God and, as far as I know, hasn't wasted a minute worrying about whether the stories in it are literally true or are fables to inspire faith. If the Bible says the whale swallowed Jonah, the whale swallowed Jonah. He is the most wholehearted believer I have ever known.

Because of those beliefs and his early training in them, the standards he sets for himself are rigid ones. He doesn't drink, never has. Doesn't smoke—although, despite my objections, he'll get into the chewing tobacco when he's with his buddies. And while we both had our jealous moments when we were young, I don't think I have ever worried about him being unfaithful.

Bobby is afraid to be bad. He believes in a literal hell where sinners spend eternity. And though his beliefs tell him you can't earn your way to heaven, that you win salvation by faith in Christ, Bobby is too scared of eternal damnation to take any chances. He is determined to be good.

Now all of that adds up to a version of Bobby Bowden that you could figure out visiting with him for an hour or two. Is that the real Bobby? Yes, it is. Since he and I have been together just about every day of our lives since I was fifteen, I think I know him better than anybody. And I can tell you that if the phrase "what you see is what you get" ever applied to anybody, it applies to Bobby Bowden.

Still, that's not all there is. Which gets us to the part of Bobby's life that most people wouldn't suspect.

The truth is, despite the fact that he seems so comfortable being so open to the public, Bobby is really a very private person. He's trained himself, through years in the spotlight, to appear totally at ease being the center of attention. It's part of the job. It's what he's learned to do to please fans and the media.

But if he had to choose how to spend an evening, it would be away from the crowds. He'd prefer to be alone with his game films or a World War II book. For company, he'd choose to be with me or maybe a few friends from high school and his college days in Birmingham. He doesn't like parties. He'll tolerate a houseful of people on game days, but, if we let him, he'll slip off to watch a game on TV by himself or with his sons.

Bobby's life has its contradictions and challenges, just like everybody else's. And like everybody else, he's been shaped by those rough spots. Yet, because he's so good at projecting the public side of himself, people seem to think he's lived this charmed life, that he came into the

world with the personality and the talent to do it all—
to become this tremendous success while "keeping it all
in perspective."

I think people who assume that aren't giving him—
and those of us who love and support him—enough
credit. He's had to work at becoming who he is. We've
had to work as a couple. And we've all had to work as a
family.

I think that more complicated version of how he and
we got to where we are is a lot more interesting than the
Saint Bobby legend that's been sort of woven around
him over the years.

That's why we've put together this book. By over-
hearing conversations between Bobby and the people he
loves and trusts the most, you'll see how the coach and
the father are mingled and how the lessons he's learned
in both roles carry over to the other parts of his life.
You'll also see, in the words of his sons and daughters,
how they've managed to absorb some of those lessons
and modify them to match their own personalities.

Bobby and I met when my family moved to
Birmingham when I was fourteen years old. We lived
close to one another, attended the same school, and
went to the same church, where I sang in the choir and
Bobby sat in the back row with the cutups.

Now, when I think about it, I can see elements of
both his mother and his father in Bobby. She was a join-
er who liked to be in charge. She taught a Sunday
school class and was president of the Federation of
Alabama Women's Clubs. His father, who was in real
estate, was outgoing, too. But he was conservative, especially about business and money.

We came along during the depression, so everybody watched their money closely. I can remember us going out with Bobby's parents on Sunday drives. We would stop for ice cream, and we would always pay for ours; they would pay for theirs. There's a lot of that frugality in Bobby, too. We've lived in the same house in Tallahassee since we moved there in 1976.

I was still a senior in high school when Bobby went off to Tuscaloosa on a football scholarship. But it became pretty obvious that life at the University of Alabama wasn't going to match up with Bobby's expectations. With all the players they brought in to compete for the different positions, he found himself in a long line of boys battling for a place on the team. Which was tough for someone who had been a high school star. Then, he missed his family—and me—back in Birmingham. He would cut classes on Fridays, because he couldn't wait to get home on weekends. There's nothing quite as powerful as young love.

Since Bobby graduated from high school at midyear, he had started at Alabama the winter term of 1949. By the spring, he was already thinking about transferring back home to what was then Howard College. And along with some other couples anxious to get started in family life, we were already thinking about marriage. On April 1, we sneaked off in Bobby's father's car to get secretly married by a justice of the peace in Georgia. I was sixteen, he was nineteen.

Now, Bobby will tell you how different things were back then, how there was so much more pressure for people who got married to stay married. But there were about five couples from our high school who made that same trip to Georgia that spring, and only one other marriage has lasted as long as ours.

I say it has to do more with the people than with the times. There was no divorce in either one of our families, and no matter how tough things got over the next few years—no matter if I locked him out of the house a couple of nights because he was spending more time with his buddies talking football than paying attention to me and the kids—we never considered divorce.

Our first child, Robyn, came along in 1951. Steve followed in 1952. Both were born while Bobby was playing football at Howard, and while we were maintaining full student lives and living with Bobby's parents.

People who hear that now always say, "What a strain on a young marriage!" And I guess it was. But we had the advantage of not knowing any better.

Once during that period, I broke out in a rash that covered my whole body. I remember the skin doctor asking, "Is something bothering you?"

There I was in our little bedroom in Bobby's parents' house. Robyn's baby bed was on one side of our bed, Steve's crib was at the foot. I had eight o'clock classes every day. I was a cheerleader, the president of my sorority. Bobby was working on campus, playing football, and serving as president of his fraternity. All this going on at once. Yet I couldn't think of a thing to tell the doctor. I couldn't think of a single thing that would be pressuring me enough to cause a rash. The truth is, we were both just too busy with each other and with our own activities to worry about anything.

By the time Tommy was born in 1954, Bobby had his first coaching job, as an assistant at Howard. Terry came along in 1956, when we were at South Georgia Junior College, Bobby's first head coaching job. The other two children, Jeff and Ginger, were born in 1959 and 1961, after we moved back to Birmingham and Bobby took over as head coach at his alma mater.

When people ask me and the children about coping with the pressures of big-time college sports, I have to remind them where we spent the first ten years of Bobby's career. In those first jobs, there wasn't any pressure—aside, of course, for the pressure someone like Bobby puts on himself to win.

There were no reporters hanging around after games. There were no coach's shows. There wasn't even much recruiting, since those small schools didn't give much in the way of scholarships and had no money for trips out of town for coaches. Bobby might have been totally absorbed in football, but he was home every night.

It wasn't until he became an assistant at Florida State University in 1963 that he was away from home much. And it wasn't until 1970, when Bobby became head coach at West Virginia, that the spotlight really fell on him. Assistants may feel the pressure, but the focus is really on the head coach. You'll hear from him directly about facing that pressure for the first time.

The good thing was, by the time we began living in that high-stress atmosphere, it was more the result of a slow evolution than of being suddenly shocked with the situation. We had the chance to adjust gradually to the increasing attention. And by that time, the kids were old enough to cope with it, too.

Bobby talks about the necessity of facing change in professional life. But adapting to changes helped us in the marriage, too. You go through different stages. You can't count on anything remaining exactly the same. If you change with them, you can work out just about anything. The trouble comes when you fight the changes. And if you let it, trouble can come when one person in the marriage is forced to adapt more than the other.

I know the biggest problem I had as a young bride and mother was the feeling that I was doing all the caring and coping, while Bobby was so busy building his career. I would get so mad that he would leave me home with those six kids and go off with his friends. That's when I would lock him out of the house.

That doesn't mean Bobby ignored his family. When we were at Howard and finally had our own house, he would come home for dinner, and while I was getting things ready, he would sit and rock the babies and give them their bottles. After we ate, I would put my feet up and he would wash dishes.

There were always outings with the kids, to the beach or someplace where we could all be together for the day. And he and I always tried to reserve a night for just the two of us, even after we had the children. It was usually on Friday nights. We would get dressed up and go out for dinner. I used to live for those Fridays. I remember we sometimes even drove the car into the backyard and parked. We still go out on Friday night dates.

But from the beginning, it was clear there wasn't going to be the kind of balance in our marriage that young brides dream of. Learning about coaching football consumed Bobby, while my life revolved around making a home for him and the kids. I just couldn't understand why he didn't feel the same way. I joke with friends now that I've never had an adult relationship: "Bobby and I started going together when we were kids, and he's still a big kid, going off with his friends to play games."

As we got older, I lost a lot of whatever resentment I had about the amount of attention he was paying to football, because I realized we were working for the same thing. We developed a division of labor. I tell him even now, "You sit up there in your fancy football office overlooking the stadium, the king of your domain. But I'm the head coach of the house."

Don't get me wrong. I'm sympathetic with women who insist that their husbands share more family responsibility. Bobby likes to tell his coaches, "You get what you demand." And I think that applies at home as well. Our compromise worked and lasted for two reasons: the foundation we had going into the pressure years; and the ambition we shared for his career.

In fact, I may have been even more ambitious for Bobby than he was. He loved the life of a coach so much in Birmingham, he might have just settled in there and stayed. But I always thought he was meant for better things. I was convinced of it. Just like I always was convinced my children were the brightest and most talented kids. I wanted him to try to move up in his profession. I wanted my children to have the chance to succeed at anything they tried.

I remember I wasn't all that enthusiastic about him taking the head coaching job at Tallahassee after his success at West Virginia. What was Florida State in those days? Nothing. Bobby was ready to go up the next rung of the ladder, and I didn't think Florida State was much of a next rung.

I think he took the job as much because of being disillusioned at West Virginia as for the opportunity in Tallahassee. In those days, he still had stars in his eyes about college football. He felt if you were a good-enough person and you tried to win the right way, that was going to be enough. Everyone would love you and support you.

West Virginia is where Bobby learned we were in a business where if you win, you can do no wrong. But if you lose, they don't care what kind of person you are. They'll forget you real fast. You'll see how Bobby—how all of us—learned those lessons of reality.

What kind of atmosphere is that for raising children? Well, remember we had a lot of time to work out family schedules and relationships before we ever had to worry about the added anxieties of big-time college football. And I think, because of the security Bobby and I felt about our lives, the kids learned to adapt.

I've had people tell me that each one of our children seems to behave as if he or she were an only child. I take that as a compliment, because I always insisted on treating each as an individual. It's so easy, when you have a big family, to just lump everyone together as being out of the same mold. Each of our kids has a distinct personality.

The two girls are very different from each other. Robyn, the oldest, is a teacher. Very even-tempered, she doesn't like to be pushed and isn't likely to push other people into a place where they are uncomfortable. I think she has Bobby's gift of making people feel at ease when they're with her. She'll go out of her way not to hurt feelings. Robyn is a mother first. And, if she and Jack could have the kind of home and financial independence they'd like, she'd probably quit working and take care of the house and kids full-time.

Ginger, the youngest, on the other hand, admits she has a T.G.I.M. attitude—Thank Goodness It's Monday. She's a lawyer, a prosecutor, who just can't wait to get to work. Like Robyn, she takes very good care of her husband and kids, but she wants to succeed on her own, too. And, like Terry and me, she's not the least bit shy about letting people know what she expects and what she won't put up with.

That gets all three of us into trouble sometimes. We have to backtrack now and then to soothe other people's feelings. But it's not that we intend to be hurtful. Some of the other kids say it's because we don't have the usual filters. If it's in our minds, it comes out our mouths.

Steve, the oldest son, is the intellectual, the only one of the boys not a football coach. For years, we thought he was going to be a doctor. Then he went to seminary and got his doctorate in philosophy. He's always been the seeker, the one in the family to try new things and new ideas. He has a wonderful sense of humor. But because he insists on analyzing things, on getting so deeply below the surface, I sometimes worry that he will have the toughest time feeling fulfilled and contented. Yet that same quality in Steve makes him a great asset. He cuts through to the heart of things, and he makes us think about what we're saying. He keeps us honest.

Tommy is the most like Bobby. He's naturally conservative and deeply religious and probably the least likely to insist on deep, hidden meanings. Like his father, he accepts a great deal on faith. He's cautious, but once he's made up his mind, he has complete confidence in his decisions. His brothers kid Tommy about being so careful, but the truth is, as a coach, he's as much a risk-taker as they are. Because he's spent so much time preparing himself, he doesn't seem afraid of anything football can throw at him. In fact, to get where he wants to go in the profession, Tommy has picked up his family and moved more than any of the rest of us. That's proof of how confident he is in his own judgment, since a stable family life is more important than just about anything to Tommy.

Everyone says Terry is the most like me. He speaks his mind so freely that he gets himself in trouble. He may be the most driven in the family and outwardly seems the most confident. Bobby has always teased him for being cocky. But I think, in a lot of ways, Terry's the most vulnerable. He is so determined to do well, he's devastated when he doesn't. He was the first of the children to go through a divorce and had a very hard time accepting the fact that he failed at something.

Jeff, the youngest son, is perhaps the most sensitive and introspective—though he'll cover it with his quiet manner around strangers and his enthusiasm for football when he's with his players. Like his father, he'll tell me in a minute if I'm sticking my nose too deeply into his affairs. Yet he's also very sentimental and affectionate. He loves to have a family around him.

Every time I hear someone at a banquet or awards dinner say something about the "perfect family Bobby and Ann raised," I get a little antsy. I guess I feel the same way Bobby does when they start that Saint Bobby business. He is no saint. And ours is not a perfect family. All-American maybe, with our children's three divorces and remarriages. But not perfect.

The one thing we may all have in common is that we like to be in charge. We're just not going to be happy unless we have a lot of say in what's going on with our lives.

Of course, what has made our children strong and independent may have also put them at risk when they were building their own families. The only models they had were the ones they grew up with. The boys, I think, may have taken for granted the idea that their marriages would automatically be like the one Bobby and I gradually evolved, that they would be free to devote themselves to their careers while their wives took full responsibility for the home and for raising the children. That's just not a fair assumption to make going into any marriage.

Consciously or otherwise, the girls prepared themselves to be the kind of wife and mother I was. Which means the risk they took was being taken for granted. And they've had to make sure to balance their own needs with the commitment they feel to home and family.

Except for Tommy, the girls had easier times finding secure relationships. Maybe that's because there are a lot more men comfortable with the traditional role of provider and authority figure than women who are happy to take a back seat in a marriage.

All of us, I think, have discovered family life in the '80s and '90s can't be made to feel like family life in the '50s. And I don't think that's a bad thing.

Every era can be the best era if you can just learn to change with the demands of the times. That's what you'll see in the following pages, a family talking about changing and adjusting.

A lot of people will try to tell you that Bobby is the last of a line, that you just can't be a person of strong faith in the modern era of sports, that you can't be open with the media and trusting of your assistants and your athletes in a world that's gone crazy with suspicion and cynicism. Well, I think people make a mistake if they think Bobby Bowden is living in some bygone age. You can judge for yourself how he's adapted beliefs he considers timeless to the challenges of a job and a family life at the end of the twentieth century. And you can see how his children are trying to carry those same beliefs into the next generation.

Part I

FAMILY MATTERS

I

THE FAMILY BUSINESS

BOBBY: When people tell me how much fun it must be to be a head football coach at a major university, this is one of the memories that immediately springs to mind:

It's 1970, and I'm at West Virginia in my first season as a head coach. We're playing Pitt. Now that game for West Virginia is the Army–Navy, Alabama–Auburn, Florida State–Florida game. It's the big rivalry. When they play "The Star-Spangled Banner" in West Virginia's stadium, the very next words out are, "Beat Pitt."

So we go out there in '70, and we're beating them 35–8 at the half. 35–8. It's going to be embarrassing. And as confident as we're feeling as coaches and players, we're not half as confident as our fans, some of whom think it's a pretty good idea to go over to the other side of the stadium and taunt some of those Pitt people. They're really laying it on.

We come out the second half and Pitt decides to play so as not to get embarrassed. They take all their wide receivers out and put in these big ol' tight ends.

Now, we had a little team. Speed, but not much size. They had a teamful of those huge Pennsylvania guys, and they figured if they could just wad it up on the line and play ball control, they might not catch up, but they'd keep us away from the ball.

They take the second-half kickoff and slowly drive for a touchdown. They go for two and get it. They get the football back, slowly drive for another one. Go for two and get that.

We can't seem to do anything on offense. They're getting all the momentum. We punt. And they get it, and here they come again. Our defense can't do nothing with that power attack. And I'm playing conservatively on offense, just the way I was taught all my life as a player and a young coach: Don't take risks, don't do anything stupid to lose the game.

Well, they go ahead of us 36–35. At the end of the game, we take a kickoff and I finally open it up. But it's too late. We get down to maybe their 40 before time runs out.

Oh my Lord, the fans just go crazy. They can't stand to lose a game like that—to Pitt, of all people, and after being ahead by 27 points at the half.

The place was bedlam. I went to the dressing room and had to go through all the interviews after the game. And there were guys beating on the door. I could hear them through the wall: "Bowden, Bowden . . . come on out of there you gutless so-and-so! C'mon outa there."

Anybody who knows me realizes there's not a fan in

the world who can feel worse about losing a football game than I do. But the way those West Virginia fans wanted my hide after that Pitt game had me scared to death. The state troopers wouldn't let me get on the bus with the team until the drunks had cleared away from the locker room doors and gone home. There is no telling what they would have done if they had gotten their hands on me.

Then I go home, and I'll never forget this. The game was probably over around five. We got out of the locker room around six-thirty. And I probably got home around nine.

I remember driving to our house, getting out of the car, and walking into the house. Ann is lying on the bed crying. She had probably been listening to the radio on the way home and heard all those things people were saying, and she just couldn't stand it. She is sobbing.

"What in the world am I doing in this profession?" I ask myself. "I don't have to put up with this. I can quit, go to Birmingham and work in my father's real estate company. Nothing's worth this kind of abuse."

After a night's rest, things don't look quite as bad. I start working with the team again, getting ready for the next game. And as soon as we win, the noise dies down. We go 8–3 that year, and I'm a genius again. This business flips and flops that quickly. Once you've gone through something like that, though, you never forget it. And it's the last thing in the world you would want to expose your family to if you can avoid it.

But here we are, a quarter century past that season in West Virginia, and I'm still in that high-pressure atmosphere. And while I certainly never planned it to come out this way, there's no getting around the obvious: College football, in one way or another, is the Bowden family business.

Ann and I had six children, four boys and two girls. I coached all four of my sons in college at West Virginia and Florida State, and I coached the two young men my daughters ended up marrying. Of our boys, only Steve chose an occupation other than coaching, and he came pretty darn close. For years, he was a college professor and administrator.

Of my sons who are coaches, all three worked under me as graduate assistants. As we write this, Terry and Tommy coach together at Auburn, and Jeff is at Florida State with me. Jack Hines, who married our oldest daughter, Robyn, is an assistant coach under Terry at Auburn.

When we get together every summer at the beach, which is about the only time we can pull the whole clan together, we end up out there in the sand sketching plays and arguing over offenses. It seems natural. But it's not exactly what I had in mind thirty years ago. It's not what I wanted; because I could foresee even then the kinds of problems we're facing now.

What if two sons were up for the same job? What if we had to play each other, recruit against each other? Well, now it's happening.

I hope to live to see the day that all three of my sons who are coaches have head jobs at major colleges—and Jack Hines, too, if that's what he wants. And I believe it's going to happen. Terry's there. Tommy's ready. Jeff and Jack will get their chances. But, man, this is not going to be an easy thing for all of us to go through.

TERRY: It's not easy, Dad. But wouldn't it have been tougher without all the help we can give one another? Think of the advantages—and I think this could be true for any family business. You can draw on people you trust almost on a daily basis. If you're not sure of something, you can run it by them. It's like you have the cumulative experience of all their years as well as your own. And not only are they tremendous resources, they are also the people who know you better and love you more than anybody else in the world. What could be better than that?

When I came to Auburn in '93, people had every reason to doubt that I was the right guy for the job. Here is this huge, tradition-filled program in the top ranks of Division I-A football. And here I am, a head coach who's never been higher than Division I-AA. I sold myself as the right guy at the right time. And I believed it. But that doesn't mean doubts didn't creep in:

"Am I really ready for this? Is there something people know at this level that I don't understand? Is this Little League stuff I've been doing to win at Salem and Samford going to work in the majors?"

That's where family becomes so important. I go to you, someone who's been more successful at this level for longer than just about anybody. And you tell me: "You can do what you've been doing, Terry. It will work. You can win."

I go to Tommy, who's been a Division I-A assistant all these years, and he tells me: "It will work, Terry." I hear that, and I've got the reassurance I need to overcome the fear that there's something I'm missing.

BOBBY: I understand that. But here's another little hitch in this family business experience. For people who aren't in this profession, for people who work in the family factory or the family store—and for your mother—there's this logical progression: The oldest child gets the top job, the next oldest probably is second in command, and so on. They move on up in succession.

But it ain't that way in coaching. You can't control the business that way. Sometimes the very best qualification you can have is being in the right place at the right time. And over the course of a career, that sense of timing is likely to come and go.

I always tried to tell y'all that coaching is like playing golf. Even if over a lifetime you're good enough to average in the 70s, you cannot go out there every day and expect to shoot 72. It will be 72, 72, 85, 80, 72, down to 70 maybe, then back up to 82. That's the way this profession is. One day you get the great job, and your brother is an assistant. Three years later it may be reversed. Or maybe you're both head coaches and one wins the national championship while the other struggles through a losing year.

All of you have watched me enough to know about highs and lows. Still, as a father, I can't help worrying. There's enough pressure already in this business without adding in the problems of competing against your own family.

TERRY: There are no guarantees in any business, even in ones that have nothing to do with competitive athletics. People end up suing one another, breaking up the business, hating each other.

It's never been that way with us, though. I'd argue, in fact, that so far it's working pretty well. Soon, Tommy will have his head coaching job. Then, someday Jeff will get his chance. Although it didn't hit perfectly the first time the way our family would have designed it, we're still on track.

ROBYN: The problem is, Terry, you have all these plans in your mind about the ways things will work out, but you sometimes underestimate the pressure on everybody else. I used to worry that you were going to burn yourself out working so hard, putting all that pressure on yourself. Now I understand that you need it, you thrive on it. You have to be in charge.

There's a whole different set of pressures on those who are in the family business but aren't in charge. It's different for Tommy. And it's especially different for Jack. If you think it's tough on brothers working for one another, think how it must be for the brother-in-law.

Jack is right there with you. To everybody else, he's one of the Bowdens, even though he doesn't have the family name. But he has to make his own place as a coach. He has to shape his own career. And while he's battling for his own identity, his own point of view, he's got to come home to his boss's sister and spend vacations with his boss's family.

Jack wasn't born to the family business. He chose it. And he can't get away from it for a moment. It's pretty consuming. And it creates so many interwoven threads in work and family relationships that it gets very complicated.

TERRY: The thing is, though, Jack may as well be one of the brothers. I don't think about him much differently. I remember us aggravating him when the two of you were dating. I can't remember Jack not being a part of the family. And I brought him with me to Auburn for the same reason I asked Tommy to stay—because I need him and trust him.

ROBYN: Everybody would expect you to say that. The good thing for us is that we know it's true. You're not just protecting family when you say it.

No matter how much you love us all and want to support our ambitions, you are not about to put yourself in a position to lose football games in order to give someone in the family a job. Too much depends on performance in this business. You have to win.

I think that's what holds this whole thing together, the prospect of all of you working together and winning. Success is the glue. It numbs all wounds. When you survive the difficulties and win, it strengthens everyone. It might have been a whole lot different if there had been a lot of losing.

Think about Tommy. When you came to Auburn, Terry, you and Jack had been winning big at Samford. But Tommy was just coming off two awful years of losing under the former coach. What he wanted more than anything was to prove that he could win again. The problem was, in order to do that, he had to take a back seat to his younger brother.

TERRY: I think that just proves my point about the advantages of working with family. Neither Tommy nor

I created the situation we found ourselves in. The question was, how could we both make the best of the opportunity? And I think that's where being brothers helped more than it hurt.

When you come into a program as big and complex as Auburn's, when you come in as a complete outsider, you've got to have somebody help you understand the politics, tell you who will be with you and who won't, who you should keep and who to let go. And that person had sure better be somebody you trust, somebody who loves you more than the school. Because if they love the school more, they'll desert you the first time something goes wrong.

What better person to have on the inside than your brother?

I could go to Tommy knowing that he would tell me the truth. He could say, "We need this guy. This guy won't work. We need to do this, avoid that." And I could believe every word without wondering if he was just trying to impress me or save his job. It made everything go more smoothly.

When it comes to the football part, we're almost in total agreement. Because the stuff we want to do is the stuff we've learned, for the most part, from you, Dad. We believe in the same things, have essentially the same priorities. So we're a majority of two, even in meetings where seven or eight other guys are on the other side.

TOMMY: Well, the truth is, you're always a majority of one. You're the boss. I'll give you my opinion if you want it, but when you say something has to be done a certain way, that's the way it's going to be done.

That's tough on an older brother, to sit there and bite your tongue when you're convinced you're right and your younger brother is wrong. I've spent my whole life as the older brother and the role of subordinate doesn't come easy.

The good thing is, these years at Auburn—especially in the '95 season, when you experienced what it's like when you don't win every week—has brought us closer than we've ever been. But I still wouldn't recommend this to most families. Work and family are probably better kept separate. I think everyone ends up being happier that way.

BOBBY: I don't know, Tommy. I may have agreed with you a few years back, but I'm coming around on this now. After spending so much of my career avoiding anything that looked like I was favoring family—probably to the detriment of a few opportunities you deserved—I've got a son as a full-time assistant coach. And I like having Jeff with me.

I'm out there in the tower on the practice field, and I see Jeff working with his receivers. He came to Tallahassee about the same age I did as an assistant. I see him talking to his players, joking with the other coaches, and I wonder if that's how I looked then. I think it was. And it makes me feel good to see him out there.

JEFF: This is where I want to be right now, too, Dad. But I can sympathize with Tommy.

I was the younger brother when I went to Salem with Terry right out of college, and it took me a couple of years to stop talking to him like a brother and to start treating him as the head coach. I had to learn to swallow a few comments, too; because I finally figured out that if I argued with Terry in front of the other assistants, it was going to affect how they all related to him. There can only be one boss.

BOBBY: You know, there were a couple of times I was tempted to fix it so that we could all be together on one staff. Once in the mid-'80s and then again in the early '90s, pro teams approached me and all but told me I could have head coaching jobs if I wanted. Before I even got out the door to meet with those guys to hear them out, you know what your mother wanted to know. She wanted to make sure I let them understand that I intended to hire my sons as assistants. And to tell you the truth, I thought that would be great.

I figured Steve could work in the front office. Tommy, Terry, and Jeff would be assistants. We could all be together working on one team. That was very, very tempting. What would have cinched it, I think, is if I thought y'all were having trouble getting the jobs you wanted at the college level—if Terry seemed stuck in Division I-AA, if nothing was breaking for Tommy or Jeff on I-A staffs. I might have jumped into the pros just to get you all into something. Then, when I retired, maybe one of you would get the head job.

Ann would have jumped all over an idea like that. But the truth was, y'all were doing just fine, moving on up in the profession. And I started thinking about something else I know about coaching: You don't want to bunch up like that in this business. You could all be out of jobs pretty dang quick.

So it came down to the same old concern, the precariousness of the profession outweighing the appeal of getting the whole family together. It's what bothered me from the beginning when y'all insisted on jumping into this business.

ROBYN: Even though Terry has a way of seeing through the "precariousness of the profession" to a future filled with nothing but success, I still think it's something worth worrying about—and planning for.

I love being in this world of college football as much as all of you. I love the excitement of the games, the pageantry. I love the competitiveness. I don't think anything can replace the thrill of those Saturday afternoons. I'm in the family business to stay, because no matter what happens, Jack is going to be coaching.

But we're all spoiled. We grew up watching you win season after season, Daddy. And except for Tommy, the boys haven't experienced much losing. It just kills me to lose. That's when I really turn to family.

Take the '95 season, for instance, when Auburn first lost to LSU, then to Florida. We fell behind Arkansas in the first half of a Thursday night TV game. Jack, of course, was in Arkansas. And I was sitting at home worrying in front of the TV set. I needed moral support bad. I called Jeff within ten minutes. I called Daddy in the first quarter. I tried to get Mother, who was at the beach.

Daddy, you said, "Don't worry, I've been in worse situations. The defense is young. They are probably doing the best they can." Jeff said, "Don't worry. It's early."

That made me feel better then, but we still lost. And

it just kills me. I can't help it. I start thinking, "This is the end of the magic carpet ride. It's all going to come crashing down."

BOBBY: Well, that's something else we all seem to have in common. We can't stand to lose.

I know it's not much consolation right after a loss, Robyn, but we all feel that way when we lose: "We've lost the magic." The difference between you and those of us who are out on the field is that we get to shake off those feelings getting ready for the next game. You have to wait until the winning starts again.

ROBYN: Life is so easy when you win. Everybody likes you. You're great. Everybody is happy. There's no friction. I don't have to face anybody at work saying "What happened?"

When the losses come, after so much success, you start thinking, "Can we beat anybody anymore? Are we good enough?" What would happen if Auburn lost three or four in a row? What would it be like for all of us? I just can't imagine.

BOBBY: I can. Which is the main reason I first resisted this idea of us all crammed into this business together. I guess it was the father in me worrying a little more than the coach in me—because I believe you all have what it takes to make it, if that's what you really want.

Back when I had you boys on my college teams, people would ask me sometimes if I could separate the coach from the father. Did I worry about you getting hurt or making mistakes you couldn't overcome? Did I feel an urge to protect you? And you know, I never felt any of that. I felt pride.

When I look back on those times, I feel like those were some of the luckiest years in my life. To have my sons out there on the football field with me, for us to be doing something that meant so much to all of us—to be at the family business—boy, that was something special. What we're doing now is about as close as we can get to what we were doing then. We're still playing the game as a family.

2

FAMILY TRAITS

ROBYN: I think there is great strength in being part of this family. When I was younger, I used to think we were a phenomenal group. We could never make mistakes. Then, the divorces started, and suddenly I realized, gee, we were doing all the normal things. We were experiencing the same sorts of things the rest of society was going through. Yet I still believe there truly is strength in being a Bowden, maybe because of the way we grew up—six children, all coming of age on college campuses as Daddy progressed up the ladder.

STEVE: Some of my fondest memories are from when we weren't very high up that ladder. Robyn, you and I have a different perspective than Jeff and Ginger, because their memories don't extend back to the earliest years of our family. My recollections are of South Georgia and Birmingham and Tallahassee up through the mid-'60s.

If I could go back and relive any part of my life, it would be those early years in South Georgia. I think we were paying $25 a month to live in a one-room building on an abandoned military base. An obsolete army tank adorned our backyard. The building we lived in had concrete floors. During the winter, when the ground was cold, we put newspapers on the floor to cover the condensation.

Adjacent to our building was another that housed the latrine. Each building had a single entrance in the front. And the two buildings were connected by a screened-in front porch. We simply walked out onto the front porch, took three or four steps, and entered the latrine door. Talk about convenience!

I used to think that *latrine* was French for *wealthy*, because none of my friends had six toilets, six sinks, and eight shower stalls in their bathrooms. Do you remember how all those toilets would overflow at the same time when only one of them was stopped up?

Honest, Dad, it was Tommy who tried to flush Robyn's Barbie doll down the toilet. Sure, I was standing there. But I was only trying to talk him out of it. I'm pretty sure it was Tommy all those other times, too.

BOBBY: Nice try, Steve. But I think my memory of some of those times is better than yours. We did have fun, though, even though there wasn't much money to go around.

STEVE: I remember Mom worked downtown at a Sears catalogue order house. In the summer, you worked the night shift at a tobacco warehouse and were a lifeguard during the day. During the school year, you were the football coach and the athletic director—and the basketball coach, too, until that year you went 1–18 and fired yourself.

BOBBY: I used to get so dadgum frustrated coaching those boys in basketball. Sometimes I'd revert to the only thing I knew. I remember getting them all in a huddle on the bench one time when we were losing by something like 20 points. I couldn't think of a single thing to say that would help them. Finally, I just blurted out, "Well, go out there and hit somebody!"

Ain't it funny what sticks in your mind?

STEVE: I recall walking home from school along the train tracks, visiting the tobacco warehouse to see the three-legged chicken on display, and having friends who came to school barefooted.

You played baseball with Tommy and me. And you took us swimming at the junior college's pool. Douglas, Georgia, in the mid-to-late '50s was that kind of small Southern town. And it was the happiest time of my life.

BOBBY: By the time we were at South Georgia, there were already four kids. It's a good thing a college campus is such a great playground for kids. I don't know what we would have done.

Nowadays, people say things like, "We're thinking about having a baby in three or four years . . . We're planning a family."

When Ann and I were coming along, we never had any idea about planning. She was sixteen and I was nineteen and a freshman in college when we got married. By the time I graduated, we had two children and another on the way. No organization, no prethought whatsoever.

My first job as an assistant at Howard College—which later became Samford University—I got $3,600 a year. And that was with a master's degree and three kids.

Planning? We just took it as it came. I was learning how to be a coach, a husband, and a father all at the same time.

ROBYN: Isn't it funny that growing up in that atmosphere, I became just the opposite. I became the ultimate planner.

When I was sixteen years old, I sat down and drew up a list of all the things I wanted in a future husband. He had to be attractive, athletic, totally dependable, and so on. Then I went out and found Jack. We started dating in high school and were almost immediately a couple.

When we got married, we planned everything. If we wanted a home instead of a trailer, I was going to have to work. If I was going to work, what kind of job? Well, teaching fit with the idea of having a family, because you can have the babies in the summer and be back to work in August. So I became a teacher, and it's worked out exactly as we planned.

Some of that may have come with being the oldest, with being Mother's representative in the house when she wasn't there. It was years before I heard my brothers and sisters talking about how they felt about that, that they considered me the family tattletale.

BOBBY: Well, I encouraged that chain-of-command idea. And I think it worked pretty well. Especially with the boys. I didn't want any one of you running in and saying, "Hey Daddy, Steve hit me."

Then I have to say, "Well, Steve, you're older. Why did you hit him?"

"Well, he was pestering me."

I didn't want to go through that with all my kids, so what I did, I got boxing gloves. And I would say, "See those gloves right there. If I ever see you two spatting, we'll put the gloves on."

I knew the big one could beat the next one, right on down the line. Steve could beat Tommy, Tommy could beat Terry, Terry could beat Jeffrey. So they knew not to pick on the guy above them or we'd get the gloves out. They couldn't hurt each other. But they all knew their limits. And I think that saved a lot of fights.

TOMMY: Now, I have a pair of those boxing gloves in my house, too. It's not a bad thing to learn that when you challenge somebody and get beat you'll have to think twice about challenging them again.

Of course, there's no getting around the pecking order that just sort of evolves in a family dominated by boys. The oldest one picked on the next one. Those two ganged up on the next one. Those three beat up the fourth and so on. The kid at the end has everybody picking on him.

I think that's why Jeff is probably the toughest of all of us. He was at the end of the line.

GINGER: Don't believe that! I'm the toughest. And for the same reason. I was the youngest. I was the one everyone could pick on.

I don't remember any big battles or any animosity between you guys. But I remember lots of wrestling and fighting and a couple of bloody noses. I think Mom kicked one of you out of the house one time for beating up on a younger brother.

JEFF: I always thought Terry was the toughest of all of us. I don't remember any boxing gloves, but if we had put them on, I think Terry could have whipped all of us.

I had a lot of admiration for Terry growing up. I saw him working out with his weights down in the basement. For wrestling, he would drop maybe forty pounds after football season. You could see the commitment and the work he put into things. He was always so driven.

GINGER: Do you think we're all like that? Everybody always talks about what a driven family this is, but I don't feel that way. And I don't think Robyn feels that way.

I guess I am ambitious. I went to law school when I was thirty and had two small kids. But I think of myself as pretty laid-back.

Of course, whenever I say that, my friends laugh.

Growing up, I never felt this pressure on me in school. I think all you expected, Daddy, was for me to be good. I don't think you even looked at a report card.

Now, when I talk to my friends who are housewives, they're always worried about getting their kids in the best private schools where they teach children to read at about three or something. They're worried sick over their children's grades. I think I shock them when I say, "Hey, I was a lousy student. Now, look at me, I'm a lawyer."

JEFF: Am I that driven? Probably not. Dad, you've always said if you work as hard as you can, if you do the best that you can and it's meant to be, you'll get that job you want. And I believe that. If that's what's meant to be, I'll get it.

I love what I do, but there are other things I could do and be just as happy. Right now, I'm enjoying where I am. I had all those years in small-college programs. No money, weak facilities, sleeping in your car at rest stops on recruiting trips because there isn't enough money for hotel rooms. I've done that. Now, at least for a while, I want to enjoy the benefits of being on one of the top staffs in the country.

I was with Terry watching him kill himself to accomplish the plan he had. He would do this for a certain number of years, then move on to that, and then, by some date he had in his head, he would be a head coach at a major program. And he accomplished it all. I just can't see killing myself like that.

BOBBY: I think each one of you is a little different from the other. Because your ages naturally grouped you in twos, it was always Robyn and Steve together, Terry and Tommy, Jeffrey and Ginger. And since y'all are the closest in ages—just sixteen months apart—Terry, you and Tommy always played together. You were almost always on the same teams. But from the beginning, you had different personalities.

Anyone who knows my family, knows Tommy is most like me of all the children. Terry is most like Ann.

Which means, out of all my kids, Tommy was the most disciplined. The best kid. If you said, be in at eight o'clock, he was in at eight o'clock. Terry Bowden, now, would come in when he got good and ready.

I would say, "Terry, I'm gonna whip you." And he would say, "Hurry up and get it over with, because I'm getting ready to head out again."

When I was young, I was just like Tommy. And I'm still like that. Here I am in my sixties and I'm still afraid of policemen. If I'm driving down the street going fifteen miles an hour in a sixty-five-mile-an-hour zone and see a policeman in my rearview mirror, I'll get down to ten. I would just know I was doing something wrong.

STEVE: That's Tommy, too. If I could draw a picture of Tommy growing up, it would be a picture of the kid who spent a long time testing the temperature before he ever jumped into the pool. Tommy always had a cautious streak. No matter how tempting the activity might appear, he would never take the plunge if he thought it was wrong.

As kids, we would ring doorbells as neighborhood pranks. We had it down to a science. We would go to the head of the street and have two kids go to the first houses on each side, then two to the next house, and so on.

Once, after we ran the whole street, we got down to the end, and there was Tommy: "Tell me about it. How did it go?" Tommy wanted to be close to the scene, but he wasn't about to risk getting caught by some irate adult roused from sleep.

Don't misunderstand, now. Tommy will take risks as quickly as anyone else. All you have to do is watch him develop an offensive game plan to know how bold he can be. But in his personal life, he is the least tempted to challenge the bounds of propriety.

Terry, I think, is driven to be like you, Dad. Tommy doesn't have to try. He is the rule–abiding one who always colors between the lines.

But there is a big advantage in being the conventional kid who becomes the conventional grown-up. You don't have to waste a lot of energy fixing the mistakes you make outside the boundaries.

Tommy leads a very self-possessed life. He knows what he does well. And he knows when he's done the right thing. As a coach, he's not tormented when he loses. It bothers him, but it doesn't send him into a tailspin of self-doubt.

Terry, because he always seems to risk more, may always have more at stake.

BOBBY: The first time I got a real strong indication of how different Tommy and Terry were must have been about 1959. I had been coaching down at South Georgia College, then got the head coaching job at Howard College, my old alma mater in Birmingham. This is about the time Howard got a brand-new swimming pool with a high dive. And my kids have never been on a high dive before. So I'm trying to teach them to jump off it.

Tommy is five or six, Terry is a year younger. I take Tommy and Terry to the pool, where I was also a lifeguard. And they're out there in their swim trunks, climbing up that ladder to get on the high dive. I'm over on the side of the pool encouraging them.

"Now boys, you've got to go jump."

So those two little kids get up on that high dive for the first time, and since Tommy's the oldest, he's got to go first. He goes out there on the end and just stands there.

I'm saying, "C'mon, son, c'mon. Jump. It won't hurt. C'mon, now."

But he won't move.

So I say, "Tommy, I'll give you quarter if you'll do it."

Well, he studies it a little more. Then, finally he jumps.

Now, he's still on his way down, and here comes Terry. Terry doesn't even give his brother time to clear. He doesn't look down to see if Tommy survives this thing or even where he landed. He just runs right off the end.

Tommy, I had to bribe. But Terry never gave a thought to the consequences: Did it hurt? Was his brother okay? He just went right off.

The first time we took Terry to the beach as a child, it was the same thing as the diving board. He ran into the water like he was heading to Cuba.

I'm yelling, "Terry, come back, come back, it gets deeper!"

But that's just him.

STEVE: I remember Terry at that age, too. Because, as the oldest, I was usually the first one off that diving board. I would still be coming up from my dive while Tommy was pondering his move. And off would come Terry. Once he landed right on my head, nearly knocking me unconscious in the water.

There's something both admirable and dangerous in that damn-the-torpedoes determination of Terry's. He has always insisted on being recognized and appreciated, on being right there with the big kids.

When we would all play tackle football in the neighborhood growing up, none of us older boys wanted to have the little ones around. When Terry was five, I was ten, and he would be right there with me and my friends. The thing was, though, when it came time to pick teams, after the first two or three best big kids were chosen, we would always pick Terry.

Everybody wanted Terry; because if you gave him the ball, he would put his head down and run without the least concern for getting hurt. It was like he could feel no pain. He just didn't care.

TOMMY: Well, he's still putting his head down and bulling his way through things. I can vouch for that. And that law degree didn't do much for his willingness to listen to somebody else's argument. You say the sky is blue, he's ready to prove it's black. He'll argue with a stump.

But I'll say this in his defense: That take-no-prisoners determination has served him pretty well. He was thirty-six when he took over at Auburn. We went 11–0 that first year, and lost only one game the next. I was the slow-and-steady Bowden who may have been on the way out of Auburn if my little brother hadn't come in to save the day. So there's not much in his experience to argue against his style.

BOBBY: Terry, don't you think some of that comes from always being the little guy? I've heard people argue—and I think I agree—that little guys are more aggressive, more determined to prove themselves. It's the Napoleonic thing. It explains some of the competitiveness in both me and you. We both always insisted on playing with the older boys. And we both were almost always the smallest guys on the field.

Growing up, there was always this instinct in me that I had to physically whip the guys who were a year or two older than me. It was like I had to be the king of the neighborhood. I would stay away from the big guys who were three or four years older, but I would challenge those who were close to my age. I had to show them that I could beat them. I had to be tougher.

I got over the need to physically beat other boys in fights. But I don't think I lost much of that need to show I could hold my own, that I could win against top competition. I just redirected it.

TERRY: I think a lot of my determination does come from being small, just like you, Dad. The thing is, though, I may be even more driven and certainly more impatient. I am you and Mother mixed together.

My willingness to take risks to get what I want has worked for me, and it's worked against me—just as Tommy's super-cautious approach has worked for him and against him. The traits that make us successful can also be our undoing.

There were many days in the '95 season, when we experienced that early loss at Louisiana State and we were fighting to redesign our offense, that I would have traded places with Tommy. I envied his approach. I have a lot of respect for the way he solves problems.

For me, it's always been about proving I can be the best, that I can win the race. Other people say things like that, but the ambition may not be as controlling a factor in them as it is in me. To say I want to be the best in whatever I do is not just an offhand remark. I'm going to find a way to organize my life to put myself in position to do just that.

I wanted to be the winningest coach ever to coach at Samford. I want to be the winningest coach to ever coach at Auburn. I want to be the winningest coach to ever coach in college football. And I'm going to try to systematically direct my life toward that.

While all that sounds great, here's the hard question: Why do something that requires all this energy and single-mindedness, often to the exclusion of so much else in your life? Is it a need to be famous? An underlying insecurity, where you've got to prove to people how good you are to be happy with yourself?

I don't know.

I'm not ready to say at this point that I'm going to be the most successful, or the happiest, or the best coach. Or that the kind of success I'm chasing is what makes you the best. It might make you win the most. But it might also make you unhappy. It might make it more difficult in your marriage, more difficult for people to get close to you or for you to go to sleep at night feeling satisfied. And there's got to be some kind of satisfaction, some sense of fulfillment for all of this to be worthwhile.

BOBBY: The problem is, son, I'm not sure the questions you're asking yourself have answers. You want it all. You want to compete at the top of your profession. You want to beat everybody at everything. Then you say you want to be the best son, the best husband, the best father, the best friend. Those are great goals. But I just don't see how you're going to work it all in.

You've picked one of the most demanding professions there is. You are a young coach trying to establish yourself at a school that's been playing football over a hundred years. You're going to have everybody and your brother telling you what you're doing wrong every time you fail to score. And Lord help you if you slip up and lose a few games.

When things get tough, about your only option is to put your head down and charge, just like you did as a kid running that football in neighborhood pickup games. Somewhere along the line, I hope you've learned from my experience that you've got to run smart as well as hard. You've got to motivate your staff and your players. You've got to keep fans interested. You've got to stay on the good side of the university administrators and the boosters. And while you're doing all that, you've got to hold together a marriage and a family.

That calls for hard work, which fortunately is something that we in this family seem to be good at. If there's one thing that connects all of us, it's that trait—dogged perseverance. When all else fails, we work hard.

All of you boys in coaching know that. Steve, who has a Ph.D., knows that. Robyn, who has a master's in teaching and is up to her ears in parenting and in supporting Jack in Auburn football, knows all about working hard. Ginger is a wife and mother who is off on a law career.

But the thing is, every time you bear down to succeed in one part of your life, you end up paying less attention to something else. There just ain't no getting around it. You're asking tough questions about how much is too much, about where you draw the line between dedication and being so dadgum obsessive about your work that you start to lose touch with other parts of your life.

I'm proud of you for asking those kinds of questions. They're important ones, every one of them. When you come up with some answers, you be sure and share them with me. We'll be on to something bigger than winning football.

3

THE COMPETITION ADDICTION

BOBBY: When you hear your children are thinking about going into coaching, the thing you worry about is, are they doing it for the right reason? I sure didn't want them to do it to please me. And when you come right down to it, there's only one good reason. Coach Bryant used to say, "Don't go into coaching unless you just can't live without it." And I'm convinced that's true. If you can't live without it, heck yeah, you'd better do it. Because you'll never be satisfied otherwise.

So when y'all started talking about coaching, my attitude was, "Boys, if you feel that the only way you're going to be happy is if you're coaching I want you to do it. But if you think you'd be just as happy in law or medicine or banking, I kinda hope you go that way. At least then we wouldn't be competing against one another."

TERRY: Well, competing against one another is not something we have as much control over as we'd all like. But the idea of competition is definitely the attraction.

Being put into a situation where I've got a group over here, you've got a group over there, and only one of us is going to win—I love that. Instant gratification. Instant satisfaction.

Now, I think that coaches who succeed over time also have other strong qualities, qualities that keep on having an impact after players' careers are over. I don't think you can last if you don't have some of that. In fact, I think you're abusing your position if you don't commit yourself to improving your players' chances at life, to helping them move from fearful, immature teens to mature men. But if we're honest with ourselves, that's not what draws us to coaching. I think the best coaches are the ones who are there because they want to compete and they want to win.

BOBBY: And because they want to compete and not lose. I don't mind telling you that's always been my motivation. I can't stand to lose. It just kills me. And because of that I might do anything. Anything. Throw the ball off my 1-, your 1-, anybody's 1-yard line.

It was that way when I used to take an underdog team into somebody else's home field where they were outmanned and overmatched. And it's continued to this day, when we run out there just about every Saturday afternoon as the team to beat. My basic approach is still the same. I am still afraid of losing. And I'm going to work hard to make sure I'm not going to lose.

TOMMY: But even after losing, after the pain of that—and my first two years at Auburn taught me all I want to know about losing—there is still something that pulls you to the game. It's the challenge. It's the chance to compete on a field where there will be no doubt who the winner is and who the loser is, where it's all laid out there for everybody to see. How many people get to do that in other professions—or would want to?

The thing is, it's something you feel called to. At least I feel called to it. This is what I think I was meant to do.

BOBBY: Ever since you were in high school, Tommy, we knew you were probably going to be a coach. I think we even have term papers you wrote back then about wanting to coach.

Jeff, the youngest, probably had the bug from the beginning, too.

JEFF: I may have had it early, but I don't think I knew it.

I wasn't all that gung ho about football when we were in West Virginia. I remember being in junior high and being more interested in hunting. The enthusiasm for football came in high school, then at Florida State. But I don't think I considered it much of a career opportunity until Terry tricked me into going to Salem with him.

At Florida State, I was majoring in criminology and figured I would end up as a Secret Service guy or an FBI agent. I could really see myself doing that. I wanted to be where the action was. But I wasn't all that great a student, as you may remember. Like a lot of players we have now, what kept me in school was my love for the game. Then, suddenly, I had enough credits to graduate. And along came Terry with his promises of what I would get at Salem—promises that, of course, never came true. But I had no expenses to worry about, and I was anxious to get back to West Virginia, where I had so many good memories growing up.

Once I got into coaching, I realized how much I liked it and how easily I took to it. Nobody else seemed surprised, because I guess they saw that in me all along. And when I look back on it now, I see the signs that signaled I was headed in that direction.

One of my earliest memories of competition is from the fourth grade, where I organized a dodge ball team. I remember sitting in school and analyzing each position on the team, then putting just the right person in that position when we went out to play. We won the championship. So maybe it is in the blood.

STEVE: Not necessarily. Despite being the oldest son, I never did consider coaching, even though I played sports throughout my childhood. And I'm going to take issue with some of your reasoning about the attractions of competition.

I'm not sure you all got into coaching simply because the idea of competition was so crucial to your identities. I suspect you're there for many of the same reasons that the children of ministers, policemen, and lawyers end up in the family business. So many kids follow the paths of their parents without even noticing it. It's not a conscious choice. The inclination is there because it's what you know best. You live and breathe in a football environment. You witness Dad's success as a coach. And you just wake up one day to find you've made a series of decisions that put you right there.

You guys are good at what you do. You are all very competitive. And now, as coaches, you can test yourselves against the best competition. You can measure your skills against the skills of other successful coaches and establish your own identity.

Everything you say about finding exhilaration and enjoyment in competition is true. But I'd wager that your strongest motives for getting into coaching are much deeper than any competitive urge.

Since I'm not in coaching, I suppose I can be more straightforward about the downside of competition in your profession. Football itself is a zero-sum game. For someone to win, someone else must lose. That's okay, because football is just a game and winning a game isn't everything.

However, we all know that at the level where all of you are competing, winning matters more than anything to the fans and to the people who hire and fire coaches. Ultimately, in the public eye, it doesn't seem to matter how well coaches live their lives or how well they relate to their players. It doesn't matter about the positive impact a coach has on his players' lives, or about values for life that players learn from their football experience.

No one wants to admit this, of course. Everyone naturally would like to have a successful coach who is also a paradigm of virtue. But it's not a job requirement. To find out what matters most, look at the bottom line: If you lose too many key games, you're gone. Imparting

virtue is nice, even laudable, but only winning is acceptable.

You guys all recognize this liability. I'm proud that
Dad has managed to win without sacrificing his good
character in the process. And I'm proud to see each of
you following in his footsteps. But if there's any reason
you're able to resist the temptations of the profession, it's
not because of the inherent values of competition, it's
because of who you are inside. And that's the quality
that's most vulnerable when you invest too much in the
outcome of games and seasons.

I suppose one thing that attracted me to medicine, to
the ministry, and to education is that they are not zero-
sum games. If you do your job well, everyone wins.
There are no losers.

BOBBY: Boy, Steve, you've hit on some of the most
worrisome things about taking the idea of competition
to extremes. I think you have to be concerned about
that win-at-all-costs mentality all the time. But I'm convinced you don't have to be that way. And I hope my
career and the careers your brothers are building help
prove that.

There is no doubt you can listen too closely to your
competitive urges. You have to develop a pretty good
sense of the time and place to really let them go. But
we've all got those competitive urges. Especially in this
family.

I think your competitive tendencies have served you
pretty well, Steve. You were always a good athlete. And
the ironic thing is, if any of the boys were a natural at
coaching, it's you. You're just such a good teacher. And

so much of coaching is teaching. But it sure didn't break my heart to hear that you were interested in being a doctor or a preacher.

Terry, for a long while, I thought you were escaping, too. When you finished at West Virginia, you came down to be a graduate assistant with me at Florida State and to go to law school. When you started law school, I said to myself that you were going to wake up and realize what you needed to be doing. You were going to be a lawyer. I kept thinking that the whole time you were with us.

Then, when you got out of law school, you immediately took the head coaching job at Salem. I mean, immediately.

With you going to Oxford and everything, I was thinking, man, you're going to be a good lawyer. Thank goodness, we won't have to be competing in this profession against each other. Then, when you took that Salem job, it was obvious what you really wanted. And now I can see where you had the whole thing meticulously planned.

You would play here, go there, get the law degree, because it would help to do this; go to Oxford because it would get you that. It's just one step right after another. You had a plan.

TERRY: Maybe that's one way the competitive streak comes out in me. Once I know what I want, I'm going to find a way to get it. I'm going to organize myself for that goal.

STEVE: Yes, Terry, but there's that other side of you—the compulsive side—that's also been one of your trademarks. I remember you getting up at four-thirty in the morning every day in West Virginia to deliver news-papers. You'd work hard, save your money, then spend it all on something you thought you really wanted—like a kayak! You'd have fun with that kayak for a while. Then it sat in the backyard until you sold it and went on to the next thing.

When you finished college and enrolled in law school, I think a lot of that was a noble effort to please other people. Being a football coach is what you really wanted. Like that kid who got up at four-thirty in the morning for your paper route, you'd go to law school all day, break down football film half the night, study until dawn, and start the whole thing over again.

You nearly killed yourself trying to please others while pursuing your love of football. The master plan theory sounds nice, but I think you needed to be a foot-ball coach. You just weren't ready to declare it in those days, maybe not even to yourself.

TERRY: We're back to this again. And I know it's both a problem and an advantage for me. I've always had a drive to be the very best—whether it was in school, where I had to make as close to all A's as I could; or in sports, where I had to win. In a family of Type-As, I may be the most driven of all. In my life so far, I seem so concerned with setting my goals high—and going after them—that they keep dominating my agenda.

I'm proud of the way I've gone about it. I'm proud of my life. But it remains to be seen whether my drive can carry me to all my goals and if it's the right kind of drive to take me where I want to go.

TOMMY: It's not just an issue for Terry. It's an issue for everyone who does this for a living.

Anybody reading this must be wondering where the pleasure is in all this compulsiveness, this drive to compete. Is this a healthy way to live?

Maybe the only honest answer to that is, "No, it isn't."

After you've been at this awhile, even the joy of winning doesn't make up for the pain of losing. The hurts go deeper and last longer.

But it goes back to getting something out of coaching you can't get anywhere else. There's a potential for satisfaction you just can't replace.

TERRY: Exactly, and I think it's important to make some distinctions between the rewards that can come with this kind of commitment and the pleasure you get from things that don't have anything to do with high-level competition. It's a distinction between *satisfaction* and *fun*.

Every season I get some kid in my office ready to quit because "football is not fun for me anymore." And I'm thinking, when was it ever fun?

It is just so satisfying. It's a measure of yourself, of who you are, what you've done, and where you're going against a standard you can't get anywhere else. The reward is in succeeding after being pushed to a level you might not have thought possible.

What I mean by succeeding is more complicated than just winning a particular game—which is one reason we say winning is only *part* of the larger game. Winning, in fact, may not be enough.

For instance: If you're beating somebody by some

outrageous score, getting everybody in the game, smiling and enjoying every moment—that might be fun. It might even be winning. But it's not football anymore. You just want to get that game over with so you can begin preparing for a bigger challenge. You know the saying: You compete in order to win, but you also win in order to keep competing.

The real goal, I think, is to be a player in the game at the highest level. To make winning last more than a game. To succeed for a season, a decade, a career.

We coaches can pat ourselves on the back for all the hours we put in. But shoot, it's the love of playing the game that draws us to it. Every coach worth his salt doesn't mind the hours at all. He shouldn't even pat himself on the back, because he can't wait for the next one.

BOBBY: I think all that's true. But when I listen to y'all talk about it, I realize the motivation in me is much simpler and more basic. It goes back to what Coach Bryant said: Don't coach unless you absolutely can't stand it if you don't.

You're right, Terry, coaching *is* playing. And I can't stand not playing. I need to be in the game.

I agree, too, that winning is only part of it; because the thing you really win is the chance to compete again, to keep playing maybe at a higher and higher level until you're at the very top.

And you're right, Steve, if you don't watch it, it can eat you alive.

I got whipped a lot trying to physically challenge

every kid anywhere near my age in my neighborhood. By the time I got to high school I was backing off that, probably because I learned to direct it into sports— where I was still determined to prove I was the toughest kid on the field.

I like to think I've mellowed as I've grown older, that I've learned to separate my competitive nature on the football field from the give-and-take that's healthy in the rest of my life. But one of the great things about making your living in sports is being forgiven for slipping up now and then and letting your competitive instincts show.

I remember one time when we were driving over to your grandmother's house in Birmingham. You boys were in the back seat. Terry, I think you were around five. Y'all had been playing with pea-shooters all day and were getting a little reckless. I think you had somehow gotten hold of some BBs and were shooting those out the window when I was trying to drive through town.

I had been scolding you, threatening a whipping if you didn't stop shooting those BBs. Just about the moment I had lost patience, along comes this guy on a motorcycle in the opposite lane. And you being you, Terry, you were drawing a bead on him. I'm in the middle of yelling, "Terry!" when, *pffffffft*, you let go. And the BB hits this guy at the exact moment he rides by.

I had already started in: "I told you to stop doing that!" And just about the second I'm trying to get the words out, I see the BB hit. "I'm gonna whip— Hey, NICE SHOT!"

Can you believe that? Here I was, trying to play the father handing out the discipline and I just can't avoid noticing it was a heck of a shot!

You know you've got the competitive sports thing pretty bad when you hear something like that coming out of your mouth. We were all lucky your mother wasn't with us.

4

SIBLING RIVALRY

BOBBY: I've always been convinced that the way we raised you children cut down on the kind of jealousies that arise in some families. There was never any of that "Daddy loves me better than you" stuff—at least as far as I could tell. For you boys, I think having those boxing gloves around helped a lot. And it probably helped that y'all were separated by ten years from oldest to youngest. But if there was ever a chance for bad feelings to slip out, for your competitive instincts to get the best of you, it could easily have been in '93 when you got the Auburn job, Terry, and you, Tommy, had to decide to leave or work for your younger brother.

When you called and told me you might have a shot at that thing, Terry, I never let on, but I just didn't think it would happen. I thought there were two things working against you. The first was my suspicion that they just didn't have the guts—and it would take guts to hire somebody from I-AA. And the other thing was the politics. I didn't think you knew enough of the right people, the ones that pull the strings on a job like that. But you had done your homework. You had met the right people, made the right calls, shaken the right hands. Knowing you the way I do, I should have figured you had that covered.

Did I doubt you could do the job? Not a bit. I knew you were ready. Just like I knew Tommy was ready. Was I afraid for you jumping into all that controversy, coming in on the heels of a scandal that put Auburn on probation for two years? Nah, we all know that perfect jobs—the ones where everything is just fine—ain't gonna come open. The ones that come open are the ones with big problems. They have to hire a problem-solver. And that's you, Terry.

I have to admit now, looking back on it, I might also have been a little worried because of selfish reasons. Alabama is my home state. I always wanted the Alabama and Auburn jobs myself. Alabama most of all, then Auburn. It never worked out for me to get either one. Over time, I came to see it as kind of a lucky thing I never did, because I never had to choose sides publicly.

Tommy, of course, got assistant jobs at both schools. And I was glad for that. But it's different when you're an assistant. The minute you become head coach of either one of those programs, everything changes; because you're bound to upset people on the other side.

Alabama is split right down the middle on football. If you're the coach at Auburn, you're going to turn off half the state, including a lot of folks you grew up with. If you're at Alabama, there goes the other half. My whole career, I never had to do that. I could go home anytime I wanted and be the fair-haired boy for both sets of fans.

I've got a million friends who are die-hard Alabama fans. So once you took over at Auburn, Terry, I knew things were going to get difficult. Oh, my old friends and I still talk and play golf and all that. But those folks know that when those teams face off against one another, I've got to go with Boy Wonder.

But the thing that gave me the most pause about the Auburn deal was the thing that's always concerned me about having three sons competing in the same profession. My first reaction was to be happy for you, Terry. My second was to think: What about Tommy? Can he handle this?

TERRY: There is no doubt that was a tough, tough time. It was difficult to find myself sitting around with Auburn people, with alumni and boosters, and all the discussion is about what I'd done and what I would bring to the university. And there Tommy is, sitting right there. It didn't feel right. It put our smaller family, Tommy and me, into greater difficulty. I don't mind telling you, at times I felt, "Hey, I don't need this."

On the one hand, I knew how tough it was on Tommy. He had come to Auburn really hot, then suffered through those two years of losing and the NCAA scandal and a head coach leaving. Then, I come in to be his boss.

But on the other hand, if they had hired someone

from a major college program, he would have brought his entire staff in, a staff loyal to him. And Tommy would have been gone. If somebody on the outside was going to get the job, the only way it could have worked out for Tommy was that it was me.

I come in. Tommy and I run the offense. We go undefeated the first year, lose just one game the second. And Tommy's a hot offensive coach again.

"Hey," I'm thinking, "doesn't anybody want to thank me?"

TOMMY: Well, I am grateful for the way it turned out. But I'm not sure anyone who hasn't been through it can understand how tough those years were.

You've got to remember the position I was in. I was thirty-six years old when I got the call from Pat Dye: "I want you to be my offensive coordinator." Everything was falling into place. I had worked my way steadily higher in the profession, until I was poised at a spot where the next logical step could only be a head coaching job at a major college. It had all been up, up, up. Then it all headed downhill in a hurry.

For someone who has pride in themselves, who has confidence . . . well, it's just so tough to find yourself back at zero. In my nineteen years of coaching, those two losing seasons were the hardest I ever worked. And there was just so little to show for it.

When you called me, Terry, and told me you were going to get the job and I could stay if I wanted, I had a very hard decision to make: go—and I had two offers to be an assistant, one on the West Coast and the other in the Northeast, at schools that had won national championships; or stay and endure and try to reestablish my credibility. I chose to stay.

TERRY: It could have been a far tougher choice for me, too—though I didn't tell you this at the time. The very first indication I got from the Auburn search committee was that if I came, they wanted to start fresh with all new people.

The NCAA had investigated, but no decision had been rendered. They were thinking: "We don't know what's going to happen to us. We'd better show we're heading in a different direction. We'd better show there have been changes. We'd better wipe the slate clean."

All I could get out of my interview discussions is they wanted me to clean house. So here's my brother, at Auburn only two years. Not a part of the old group. Not named in any allegation of rule violations. Yet he was on the slate they wanted wiped clean.

Here I am, thirty-six years old, being offered the job of my life, the job of my dreams. And the first thing they're suggesting is that I fire my own brother.

I know exactly what you're going to say about the realities of the business, Tommy. But I could never have felt comfortable with that. I had to make it clear I intended to keep some of the old staff, especially you. If I had to take a job on the condition that I summarily dismiss my brother, I don't know how we could exist as a family.

TOMMY: We didn't have to talk about this at the time. What was there to talk about? I understand what a president, boosters, athletic directors have to do.

Sometimes it isn't a head coach's decision who gets to stay and who has to go.

To be honest with you, Terry, it would have been easier if a condition of you getting the job was that I be let go. I would have understood. If you had asked me my opinion, I would have said, "Take the job, fire the brother. How often does an opportunity like this come along?"

In a way, it would have solved my dilemma. I would have had no choice but to go, instead of having to stay in an atmosphere where I knew a lot of people were saying I couldn't coach: "We were winning until he became offensive coordinator, and now the only way he can hold on to his job is because his brother is head coach."

I had a choice—which is always a good thing. But it put pressure on me.

BOBBY: About the only advice I could give you then, Tommy, was, "Don't leave just to be leaving. Football goes up and down. Be patient."

I know people accuse me all the time of failing to see the bad side of things, of always seeing some purpose in what seems like the worst kind of luck. And I plead guilty to that. It's a key to my spiritual beliefs. I believe things happen at God's pace. When God is ready for you to have that job, no man can stop you.

In the meantime, I think you ought to work the job you have as if it's the last one you'll get. Stay at Auburn, I said. Set a goal to make Terry the best head coach in the country, and you'll serve yourself in the process.

The hardest advice for any of us to take is the advice to be patient in tough times, to realize that what we're going through will make us better people. Even when things looked pretty bad, Tommy, I was sure this was going to make you a better coach in the long run. This is a plan. This is the way it's supposed to be.

TOMMY: You know I believe that, too, Dad. And it does look as if this has worked out the best possible way. At the time, though, it didn't seem headed in that direction. My brother saved my job. But it still felt like a demotion.

I had been offensive coordinator under Pat Dye. When Terry came, I lost the title.

TERRY: When I came in, I was really worried that, even if what we wanted to do worked in the long run, we might not be very good the first year. So I didn't give anybody the offensive coordinator title.

What I said was, "If you're going to blame somebody for the offense we put in, if you want somebody to blame for the play-calling, blame me. I'm the offense coordinator per se."

From the first day, though, you had offensive coordinator responsibilities, Tommy. You did all the work without a title.

That first year we go undefeated. And before the next season I say, "Hey people, I'm going to make Tommy Bowden offensive coordinator. And surprise, surprise, he's going to do exactly what he did last year."

Only in retrospect, only after you've been successful, can you tell people, "Well, I thought he was the best coordinator in the country, and he was doing the job from the time I got there—even when he didn't have the title."

BOBBY: The truth is, you both needed one another. Tommy, you needed Terry to give you the chance to prove yourself to the doubters. And Terry, you needed Tommy as an advisor and partner in the offense. Maybe neither of you could have had the success you've had without the other.

You're on the same team, just like you were growing up. I remember when you two were in the same peewee football backfield. Tommy was the tailback. Terry was the fullback. So in the I formation, the running backs were Bowdens. If Tommy gets the ball, it's Bowden right. If Terry gets the ball, it's Bowden left.

Both of you played on the same baseball teams, the same high school football team that went to the state championship. Because you were always on the same team, playing different positions, the competition between you was never that bad. It's the same way now. Even though that might not last if the next step in your careers puts you at different schools.

TOMMY: With our success at Auburn, people started talking about me as a head coaching candidate again. It's become more likely that Terry and I will be at different big-time programs soon. And chances are, we would end up facing one another on opposite sides of the field.

Would I like that? Sure. I think everybody would enjoy the hype of brother against brother. It would be great for fans. And we all realize that the guy who loses that game is not going to commit suicide.

Then, there's this to look forward to: There's still a perception out there that Terry's somewhere up there high on the head coaching talent chart, and I'm somewhere down there below him.

I wouldn't mind a chance to balance that out a little.

5

FATHER VS. SON

TERRY: If we can both hold on to our jobs, Dad, and some bowl committee doesn't match us up before 1999, that's when we'll have the first Bowden Bowl. Florida State vs. Auburn during the regular season.

When I was at Samford, you'll remember, I pushed this Father vs. Son thing pretty hard, and you wanted no part of it. Of course then it was strictly a one-way advantage for me and nothing for you. You kept saying how much you worried about beating us up. And I kept saying, "Don't you understand, it's not about getting beat, it's about bringing the spotlight to Samford?"

The object was to help our budget and bring prestige to the school.

BOBBY: Think of it from my point of view. In the first place, the Florida State people were going to know

I was doing it just to help my own son, and they weren't going to like that. Especially if we got out there and slopped up the game and risked getting beat.

Then, what if we book it years in advance—because that's how you have to set up schedules—and you leave? Then what? Here's big ol' mean Florida State picking on little ol' Samford.

Well, sure enough, that's what happened. You got the Auburn job and left. If we had made that schedule, we would have been stuck with playing a I-AA team while we're trying to convince people every year we're a legitimate contender for a national championship. The media would have had a field day, and they would have been right.

I remember telling you at the time that our athletic director had vetoed the idea, but I was lobbying pretty hard behind the scenes to keep Samford off our schedule. That's when you tried an end run. You put your mother on me.

I had to listen to Ann: "You play everybody else's son, but you won't put your own boy on the schedule to help him out!"

TERRY: And that's when you sent me the Stop-Being-a-Mr.-Know-It-All letter. Remember that? I still have it. It was in March of 1991, and you had just about had it with my pestering. This is what you wrote:

"You have become too obsessed with playing a I-A school. For a football coach working to go to the top, your top priority should be winning games. Your priority is not to balance the budget and pay the bills. . . . Quit telling other coaches and athletic directors what they need to do with their programs. . . . I don't want you to come off as a know-it-all."

BOBBY: I reckon that advice got filed with all the rest of the stuff you never pay attention to unless it suits you. Are you happy now? I've come around on this game. I think it's one that ought to be played. It will be great for the fans and good exposure for both schools. As far as I know, no father and son have coached Division I-A teams in competition with one another.

A lot can happen before 1999, though. I suspect Tommy will get his head coaching job at another school by then. Jeff and Jack could be somewhere else, too. So it could be just you and me, Wonder Boy.

TERRY: The truth is, when I got to Auburn I sort of lost my desire for the matchup. Suddenly, I'm the new head coach of a I-A team that I'm supposed to take to the same level as yours at Florida State. What if I take my kids to Tallahassee and get them thumped pretty bad? It would be: "Well, we got a Bowden. But he ain't the right Bowden. The daddy's I-A and the son's I-B."

I didn't need that when I was trying to convince everybody that we're on the brink of competing for it all. It will come for us at Auburn. But when I first arrived, despite what I was telling people to get them pumped, I knew your program had shot up there in the last five years or so, and I needed time to get ours caught up. So I became the one who didn't want the Bowden Bowl.

Then some things happened to change my mind again. You win the national championship in '93 and start talking about wanting to coach at least through the 1999 season. I go 11–0 my first year in '93. And coming off those years, both of us are feeling pretty good. I say, "Hey, we've got these programs where we want them. Let's do this thing before you finish up."

Since then, of course, it hasn't been quite as smooth for either one of us. We lose a few more games between now and then and 1999 won't look like as much fun. But we're committed. It's going to happen.

What I'm hearing now are questions from folks who want to know how we're going to handle it, how we're going to take these intensely competitive personalities into a game against one another and not let it divide the family.

STEVE: I hear those questions, too. I can understand why Dad resisted the idea when you were at Samford, Terry. Why open that can of worms?

Then again, I think all of us in the family know better than to let such competition become a divisive issue. It's just a game. You've got eleven kids on each side of the ball to see who can win. It's a sophisticated form of kick-the-can. And both father and son can benefit.

Even as the opposing coach, Dad can't help but feel pride in any of his sons' successes. And Terry gets to match wits with one of the winningest coaches in college football history. It's a can't-lose situation, as far as I'm concerned.

Of course, I don't have to deal with the unhappy alumni. And my livelihood isn't affected by the outcome of the game. But still, I can't imagine a scenario in which any serious family division arises out of a contest between father and son or brother and brother. At least, not for us. And not over a football game.

BOBBY: You're exactly right, Steve. That's what I think, too. But maybe you ought to talk to your brother Jeff about this. I think it's getting to ol' Jeff already. Or at least it's beginning to get to my staff, and they're getting to Jeffrey.

Remember that business about the game films, Terry?

TERRY: This is what happened. Early in the '95 season when we had that close loss to LSU in Baton Rouge, I felt like I needed to do something to juice up our offense. I just wasn't comfortable with the game plan we had put together. At one point during the game I remember looking down at my play sheet and thinking, "I don't like any of this. We don't have a play on here that I want."

So after the game, I did what I always do. I turned to my resources. I turned to family. I called Jeff and left a message for him to send me some Florida State offensive game film. I wanted to study your four-wide-receiver scheme to see how we could work more of that into our offense.

At that point, I was feeling a little desperate. We had just suffered our first loss of the season, only the second in three years. And we couldn't seem to get anything going on offense. I wanted help.

So Jeff calls me back when we're in our staff meeting. He says, "You want our film, you've got to send me your film."

What?

"I just want to study it," he says. "You know we may have to play y'all in a bowl game. If you're looking at our film, I want to look at yours."

So I say, "Okay, I'll send you the dadgum film." And I hang up on him.

I tell one of our graduate assistants, "Here are my car keys. You drive my car down to Tallahassee right now and hand this film to him." And I wrote this little sarcastic note: "I hope this helps y'all with Clemson."

Now, I know Jeff is getting all this from those other assistant coaches. They're good guys, but they're afraid all their secrets will get out. And they get on Jeff. But this was family. And I was mad.

My grad assistant drives three hours down there, and he walks right on the practice field and hands that film to Jeff.

JEFF: Hand-delivered, I liked that. It made me feel a little guilty, but you have to realize how I was looking at the situation.

I got to thinking, "If we end up undefeated and they end up undefeated, we could play each other for the national championship. Or if we lose one or two and they lose one or two, someone is going to want to match us up in a bowl game. Everybody's going to want to see that.

"And here we are giving Terry all our film, while we ain't seen a bit of theirs. If we have to play them, they know everything we're doing. I don't know anything they're doing."

TERRY: But I promised you this film was for our offense. I wasn't going to show it to our defense. There wasn't any point in that.

I was mad. But then you wrote me that note back.

JEFF: I said, "You taught me well all those years I was with you: Leave no stone unturned. All I was trying to do was cover every angle.

"I learned from the best."

You have to remember I've been through something like this before. When I was at Southern Miss, we played Tommy and Auburn twice. We won once, they won once.

Now, it wasn't like it was Tommy's receivers against my receivers. We were both coaching offense. But still, playing family takes a little of the edge off the pleasure. You're 85 percent happy when you win and 15 percent sorry for your brother.

Where this Auburn vs. Florida State thing is going to get intense is over recruiting. Recruiting is a war. It doesn't have to be dirty. But it's a war. And remember, Terry, I worked with you for eight years. I know how you operate.

TERRY: There is no getting around the fact that we're going to go head-to-head on a lot of kids down in Florida. There are all those great athletes and only four Division I-A schools, now that Central Florida has moved up. Those kids have to go somewhere else, and I like to tell them we're the closest big-time program to the Florida border. If they want to play on TV, in a big-time conference, with a chance to compete for a national championship—and still be close to home—they can come to Auburn.

When I give speeches I joke about the Bowden blitz on some of those top prospects in Florida. If the kid is a blue-chip receiver, in one night he might get a call from receivers coach Jeff Bowden from Florida State, then receivers coach Tommy Bowden at Auburn, then Florida State head coach Bobby Bowden, then Auburn head coach Terry Bowden.

That kid ends up so confused he might not know who he signed up with until he gets in a car in August and looks at a road map. All he knows is he's going to play for a Bowden.

There are unwritten rules I abide by, though. I don't let any of our assistant coaches tell those kids that because Tommy and I are our father's sons we have an inside track on exactly when he plans to retire. We don't go into prospects' homes and tell them Daddy's not going to be around by the time they're juniors or seniors.

JEFF: Yeah, but in interviews and booster speeches, you tease so much about Dad's retiring you keep the issue out there. You make it a factor. You say all that in fun, but when you beat us out on a couple of top prospects, it's not so funny anymore.

BOBBY: Listen to you boys. I got a kick out of that film exchange stuff, because I hadn't been thinking about 1999. But I am now.

We've always traded information back and forth. We do a lot of each other's stuff, especially on offense. We've always done that. But it's going to get to a point, as 1999 creeps up, that we won't be sharing as much as we have in the past. We ain't gonna be quite as helpful in recruiting either.

I always figured that if we can't take a boy, why not steer him to one of y'all. Since you've been at Auburn, Terry, I've been pointing kids your way, both to help you out and to keep them from signing with somebody we have to play every year, like Florida or Miami. But every kid we're recruiting now has a chance to play in that game in 1999. So I'm gonna have to quit steering boys your way.

We've got a staff here—and Jeff will lean with them— that is suspicious that there's already too much talk back and forth. And you have a staff, Terry, that probably feels the same way. Here, they think that because I'm the father I'll want you to have all this information that can help your program.

I can tell you that Jeff, for one, isn't going to have all that much compassion. He'll be like the other coaches: "Don't tell 'em anything. We've got to play those guys."

TERRY: I guess there's no way around that with the staffs. But we don't have to slip into that as family. There's no reason to believe that Florida State is going to slip much from the place it holds in college football between now and 1999. And we're building something at Auburn that should be right up there with you. The lead-up to that game could make it the most anticipated matchup in a long time. We should all enjoy it. And no matter who wins, we will all be in the same suite celebrating.

BOBBY: That's exactly the way we should be looking at it. The reason I can enjoy it so much is that it will be coming toward the end of a career that has pretty much assured me a place in the sport, regardless of how one or two games come out. If I lose to my son, they ain't gonna fire me or take away anything from the record I've established. And if we beat you, that one game shouldn't take anything away from the record you're making at Auburn. If it makes you vulnerable to criticism from boosters and fans, it means you were already in trouble.

This won't become some big rivalry. It will be just the Bowdens having a go at one another, putting a show on for the fans, before ol' Bobby leaves Florida State.

TOMMY: Now hold on, Dad. Don't start insisting this is the last Father vs. Son game. If I get a head coaching job, the least you could do is put me on the schedule, too. After all, I'm the older brother.

And how about Jeff? Don't you think we all deserve a parting shot at the old man?

I think you ought to hang in there. Maybe we can get a tournament going.

6

MEASURING UP TO DAD

GINGER: When I wrote my personal essay for my law school application, here's how I began it:

"I was born on a dark night. My mother was unconscious. My father was out recruiting. And I've been trying to get their attention ever since."

Isn't that funny? I think it's true. It tells you something about me. But it's also misleading.

There have been times in my life when everything wasn't going the way I wanted. And like most people looking around for something to blame my problems on, I pointed to my parents. Daddy wasn't around. And Mom was always overcompensating.

But you know, when I really sat down and thought about how I felt about growing up, I couldn't think of a single time I felt deprived of something. We just thought that was the way everybody lived. Daddy goes to work at five A.M. and comes home at eleven P.M. And four months out of the year he's out recruiting.

I was never one of those kids peeking through the curtains before the school play wishing Daddy was in the audience. I just thought that was the way things were. That's what we all thought. And while each one of us imagines from time to time we're head cases, the truth is, we had pretty happy childhoods.

But that doesn't mean we didn't take away powerful influences from growing up in that environment. I think all of us, in one way or another, are measuring ourselves through our father's eyes. We want to please him. And if we can't do that, we definitely want to avoid, at all costs, disappointing him.

I know I'm still doing that. And I think it's the same with Robyn and my brothers.

TERRY: People ask me about the pressure of being compared to you, Dad, as a football coach. And I tell them being a Bowden takes some of the pressure off of being compared to anybody in football. Heck, I may not even be the second or third best coach in my family. So what do I care about the argument over who's the best coach in the conference or in the nation? Any one of us sons can have wonderful careers, and it's not likely we're going to accomplish what you've accomplished, Dad.

In some family businesses, I suppose, that could drive sons away. You look at those marks, those records, and all you see are standards you may never reach. But because of the relationship we've all had growing up, I don't think any of us has ever felt we are being measured by our father's success in football.

Competing with our father's image, now, that's a whole other issue. That's probably a harder thing to deal with than the football. Certainly, it's the thing that has given me more sleepless nights.

Maybe it's because none of us see ourselves as being as good as other people. Surely, we know our own faults better than those around us. But I worry a lot that I can't live up to the public image you've established over the years. I don't see myself as being the kind of role model you've become, the Christian leader that you are.

Although I know that image is not something you've actively cultivated, it's become a major part of who you are to millions of people. And because we're Bowdens, it's become part of the way people perceive us as well.

ROBYN: That sense of falling short of the image shows up in even the most day-to-day routines. I've been so busy with the children lately, running all over the state with soccer competitions and their school activities, plus my own teaching responsibilities, what's suffering right now is my church attendance. Come Sunday, I am just so tired.

It's the one day I have to catch up on my rest and to organize the family for the week. But I'm really wrestling with that. That's not how I was brought up. And I know, because my father is Bobby Bowden, people, especially in a small town like Auburn, expect me to be in church. Around here, the second question they ask you is where you go to church.

If I was Joe Blow, people wouldn't notice. But because I'm Bobby Bowden's daughter, I feel guilty—not because I've chosen to stay home on Sundays, but because I'm not living up to my father's image.

TERRY: In one important sense, having the name Bowden is one of the greatest things you can have going for you. It's like having a professional degree. It immediately gives people a presumption about you. In law school they tell you that having a presumption is the most important thing in a case, because it's the other side that has the burden of proof.

If you have the presumption of innocence, it's up to the prosecution to demonstrate otherwise. When you have a law degree, people assume you're pretty smart, that you can handle yourself in a competitive business environment. When you are the son of Bobby Bowden, people presume you have his genes—not only that you can coach like him, but that you're just as good a person as he is, that you've always been able to uphold the same standards. And that's where the guilt comes in.

I don't have any problem with football expectations. In football, all the presumptions of excellence in the world get you nothing without performance on the field. No matter what anybody says, I can't ride my father's coattails for long when it gets down to actually playing the games. But since people aren't tested in the same clear-cut way in other parts of their lives, presumptions about my qualities as a man, a husband, a father, a Christian leader aren't challenged in the same way. And it's too easy to be a hypocrite.

I know I'm not a bad person. I may be better than most. But alongside my father . . . Well, I can look into my heart and see my failings, how I don't measure up to being the kind of role model you are, Dad. People presume: "Look at that Terry Bowden, he's a chip off the old block. His father's son."

And sometimes I feel that if I allow those presumptions to persist I'm silently endorsing the mistakes I've made, whether it's my divorce or some other shortcomings.

BOBBY: I'd hate to think that at this late date y'all are all caught up in the Saint Bobby business. Of all people, y'all should know better.

The folks who started calling me Saint Bobby were the ones who put a little twist in their voice when they said it. I think they were mostly Gator fans. But they definitely did not intend for it to be complimentary.

I've been fighting that goody-goody stuff for years, because if you let people make you out to be perfect there just ain't no margin for error. I tried to joke it away at first. I told people that the trouble with having that halo hanging over my head was that it wouldn't take much for it to slip down and become a noose around my neck. And that's exactly what happened after we won the national championship in 1993 and the Foot Locker scandal broke.

Some kids took shoes and clothing from agents against NCAA rules, and you would have thought they had discovered Murder Incorporated on the Florida State campus. *Sports Illustrated* runs a cover story saying our national championship is "tainted," and I've got reporters swarming all over me asking, "How come you didn't know this was happening? Aren't you Saint Bobby? Aren't you supposed to know everything?"

Two years later, I get hit with the same kind of thing,

this time from a writer from *The New York Times Magazine,* whose story implies we're a bunch of hypocrites for professing to be so saintly and yet running a program where players sometimes get in trouble.

Now, in one sense, I guess I've invited some of this stuff by promising to have as much influence on these kids as I possibly can. I tell parents that I'll do my best to be like a parent to their boys, that I'll watch over them and, when necessary, discipline them the same way a father would. But I've never claimed to be so perfect and so powerful that any player on my team is going to be immune to every temptation. Some are going to mess up, just like we all mess up from time to time. Some, unfortunately, are going to get in serious trouble—no matter how much we watch over them and preach to them.

The only thing that makes our kids different from others their age is that they're on a football team that is in the national spotlight. Joe Smith college student can get arrested for drunk driving or for getting in a fight, and the story ain't going to be on ESPN or in the sports pages the next morning. No one is going to be insisting the university kick him out. But the rules are different for our coaches and kids. It's part of what changes when you have great success and everybody seems to know who you are.

All this puts my staff and players under a terrible strain. They know if they mess up, everybody's going to come back and say, "Ol' Bowden ain't livin' up to his image." And now I hear my own children worrying about the same thing.

You want my advice? Don't worry too much about

what others think. It will paralyze you. Focus on what you believe to be the right path. And when you stumble or wander, don't give up. Pick up where you left off and start again. If you're heading in the right direction and you work hard enough, success eventually will overcome all the criticism. But if you react to every little thing, you'll bounce around forever.

Terry, when you say you look into your own heart and find all these shortcomings, don't you know that everybody else feels the same way? We are our own best experts on our failings.

When I look back on my life, I remember things I'm ashamed of. I don't broadcast them. My sins are between me and the Lord. But I have regrets.

In my younger life, I may have been too wrapped up in my own career to pay attention to kids who were not great athletes but who needed guidance. I might have run kids off from some of my teams to make room for others with more talent. I'm not proud of doing that.

I think, if I were to do it all over again, I'd change some of the things I did as a parent, too. When we were bringing y'all up, I was so concerned with not saddling you with the "Bobby Bowden's kid" thing I may have shortchanged you in the process. I didn't want anybody to think you had gotten something just because you were mine. So I made it harder on all of you.

When Tommy was a senior in high school, he was a wideout and a defensive back. He was a terrific receiver. There was another wideout on his high school team who was pretty good, too, but not really half as good as Tommy. When they graduated, I gave the other kid the scholarship and didn't give Tommy one—even though Tommy was better. I just thought too much would have been said about him being my son. But I know that hurt Tommy.

Now, both these kids went to West Virginia, and Tommy beat that kid into the ground. But I made him wait two years to get a scholarship. I made him play defense in practice where he got his brains beaten out.

I know I did the same thing with you, Terry. I didn't give y'all anything.

I figured I could have handled the criticism from fans who thought I was favoring my own kids, but I thought if I brought you in immediately you might not have been accepted by the team. "There goes Daddy's boy," they'd say.

TERRY: We got that anyway, Dad. You hear, "Well, he got that job because he's Bobby Bowden's son."

Even in situations where that might not be the case, it's still the first thing that pops into people's minds. I found the easiest thing to say is, "Yeah, I got every job because I'm Bobby Bowden's son. I got every job because he taught me football since I could understand English. I got to sit around the breakfast table and hear him talk about problems and what he had to do to handle them since I was a kid. Because I was raised by him, I was able to coach Auburn at thirty-six years old. Yes, I got every job because I was Bobby Bowden's son."

That's my way of saying I see the family connection as adding to my qualifications instead of taking away from them. Still, there are still going to be people who don't see it that way, who see an opportunity that opens to me as something completely unearned. To them, the only thing I can say is, "Let's wait and see."

GINGER: What you taught us about creating our own identities is important, Daddy.

When it came time to fill out my law school application, the Bowden name was one of the most famous in the state of Florida. But I went out of my way to keep every reference to my maiden name and to you off my application. That was very important to me, to make it on my own.

When I hadn't heard back from the admissions people and we were already into the summer months, I finally mentioned it to you and asked if you could check on it. But before you could talk to anybody, I got my acceptance in the mail.

When I started law school, I found out that most of my classmates had made it in by knowing somebody—a dean, a big lawyer in the state, a judge. But I was so proud I did it my way.

BOBBY: I'm glad that turned out. And I'm proud of what all of you have done on your own. But if I had it to do over again, I would give Tommy that scholarship. I would give Terry and Jeff more opportunities to play. I would help the rest of you along a lot more than I did. I would lighten up a little.

That's pretty good advice, isn't it? Lighten up.

Robyn, I know you must feel guilty about not going to church when you need to stay home and rest. We were all raised with that Sunday church habit. But whatever you feel should not be based on the image people have of me, or even on what you think of my faith or your mother's dictates. It should come from you. You keep your personal relationship with the Lord right, and church will take care of itself. Sunday, after all, is the Day of Rest.

I think y'all have to be careful about measuring yourself against some image you or others have created. You'll always fall short. And you'll always be punishing yourself.

There's only one person who's ever been perfect on this earth, and He ain't your daddy.

7

MEN, WOMEN, AND FOOTBALL

TERRY: If there's one area of my life where I feel I haven't measured up to my own expectations—and to my family's—it's this one: My brothers and sisters and I have parents who have been married almost fifty years, who have these strong spiritual values that helped them stay together all that time. What better example could I have? And yet I couldn't hold my first marriage together.

I can rationalize it, saying, "Well, these are different times. Men and women bring different expectations to marriage now. And when things get tough, society makes it easy for you to give up and get a divorce. Too easy."

Yet that doesn't stop me from feeling guilty. I've always had the attitude that if I tried hard enough I could be successful at anything I wanted. Marriage is something I wanted to succeed at and failed. And that stays with you your whole life.

BOBBY: I know it does, Terry. But I'm not sure you're going to accomplish anything by punishing yourself with the memory of failure. You are such a perfectionist. The way you plan out your life, you certainly wouldn't have planned a divorce into it. But this is not an unpardonable sin.

You know I believe that marriage is sacred, that God meant us to have only one wife. When husbands and wives have problems, they should realize that their problems are no worse than those their fathers and mothers had, or their grandfathers and grandmothers. Those disagreements are just part of married life.

I don't believe God wants us to divorce. But if we do, I don't believe He turns away from us either. Everything I understand about the Bible suggests He will pardon us for our mistakes. And I think He wants us to pardon ourselves, too—provided we learn from our experience and avoid making the same mistakes again.

I don't care when you get married, what era you live in, there's nothing easy about marriage. You've got to work at it. It truly is work. But it is a fact that when your mother and I were coming up people just didn't divorce as often. There was a stigma to it. And there's no doubt there's an advantage in that. If you don't consider divorce an alternative, you pretty much have to work things out.

I can remember, before we had any children, Ann and I would fight just about as hard as any couple ever did.

We got married young. And we butted heads over lots of things. Often it would be about money or about one or the other of us looking a little too long at somebody else. There were times in those days that Ann and I would be having some spat and she would start packing her bags.

I would be standing there arguing with her and at the same time pleading, "Ann, please don't go, please don't go." And thank goodness, she never did. But nowadays I think young people in that same situation would leave and not get back together.

TERRY: It's even worse when you're caught up in building a career, especially a career that clearly brings you so much satisfaction. When you're married to your job, it makes your wife the jealous mistress.

I slipped into it without even knowing it. Football was the essence of my daily routine. It started in law school, when I was a graduate assistant in football and also the dorm manager. I managed all the athletic dorms. To make some money, I was a bouncer at a Tallahassee restaurant from eight P.M. to two A.M., Thursday through Sunday nights. And I was running eight miles a day training for a marathon. My wife never saw me.

We got married when I was still in my second year of college. And when we moved to Tallahassee, I took her away from her home in West Virginia, where all her family was. Then, I got wrapped up in a schedule that had no place for her.

I think I just assumed that was what a wife had to do. She just had to bear with it. My mom had to go through it. She had to raise six kids while my dad was out trying to learn how to be a coach. That was the way things were.

That may have been the one situation in my life where applying the lessons I absorbed at home worked to my disadvantage. The '80s weren't the '50s.

BOBBY: Well, times have changed. But this was never an easy profession on wives who expect you to be home all the time. You'd better marry someone who understands that, or there will always be problems.

Back when Ann and I got married, most folks just assumed it was the husband's responsibility to make the money and the wife's to stay home and take care of the family. But you know your mother well enough to know that, even if she was willing to accept that role to a certain degree, she wasn't going to be shy about making demands. She always had pretty strong notions about how this marriage was going to work.

I always thought I was lucky, too, that in the first ten years of my career I was at Howard, then South Georgia, then back to Howard—both little schools that couldn't afford to recruit much. And we didn't have a lot of film of opposing teams to study in those days. So while I might be working long hours at football during the day, I was home every night with Ann and you kids.

Even if y'all were in bed before I got home, you saw me the first thing in the morning when you got up. In that way, maybe we had a jump on a lot of modern families who may be better off financially, but where the father is away from home for long stretches on business.

When I went to Florida State as an assistant coach in

'63, I think I was down there three weeks or so before y'all could make the move. It was the longest Ann and I had ever been apart.

Later on, when I started going on long recruiting trips for a week or so, Ann wasn't all that happy about me being away. I would try something like this out on her: "Look, when Daniel Boone would take off for the west, he'd be gone for a year. And his wife and children had to stay behind in that little cabin in the woods surrounded by all those Indians." But I don't think your mother was buying into that.

What helped us, I think, was that Ann always had a lot of ambition herself, ambition for the family. She wanted me to succeed. She wanted the family to prosper. It wasn't like she was happy living on that old army post down in South Georgia where I started coaching. She got a pretty good look at the governor's mansion and figured that would do just fine somewhere down the line. So she was always supportive of bigger and better opportunities.

She and I made every important decision together. Every time I was offered a job, the two of us would sit down and talk a long time about it, weighing all the pros and cons. And she had as much say in whether I took it as I did.

TERRY: Maybe that was one of the lessons I wasn't paying as much attention to. In my first marriage, there could have been a lot more honest talk about what we wanted out of life, both together and individually.

When I graduated from law school and took the Salem job, I thought it was the best thing for both of us.

But she probably had a different perspective. I thought: Salem was forty miles from where we were raised in West Virginia. I would get to coach, she would be near family.

The problem was, I had signed on for a job that made success look beyond the realm of possibility. And as far as my time was concerned, it was Tallahassee all over again.

I had no money, no paid assistants. Just a bunch of volunteers. There were no washers or dryers. So every night after practice, I was out at laundromats, stuffing practice jerseys and shorts into six machines to wash and dry them for the next day. It just got tougher and tougher on the marriage. I could promise her I would change. But I couldn't really. I kept thinking, "Hey, this is what it's all about!"

The more desperate I thought the football situation was, the harder I worked at the office. I was doing everything. I was academic counselor and financial aid director for the players. I was the head recruiter with no full scholarships. And Salem was paying me all of $16,000 to be head coach. For her, the obvious question was, "Why did you go to law school if this is what you intended doing all along?"

Her father was a lawyer. He probably planted the seed in me to consider law school. I thought it would look good on my résumé. But I think she always had that deep-down hope that I was going to get away from football and be a lawyer like her dad.

BOBBY: Well, you know, son, that's what a lot of us thought you were going to do. Until you grabbed that

Salem job, we didn't see you jumping into coaching with both feet. Maybe we weren't paying as much attention as we should have been to what was really going on inside you. But chances are, you weren't being all that clear about your intentions, either.

TERRY: Deep down, I guess, I was fearful that she would never accept my football. Or that she would always be unhappy that I was putting so much into the game. I was too afraid that she wouldn't be accepting of who I was.

ROBYN: Before you two even got married, I remember talking to her during one of your fights. I was sympathetic, because I could see how she viewed the problem: You were ignoring her.

What I told her, though, was that, no matter how much you promised to change, there was a pretty good chance that's who you were. You weren't going to turn out to be this entirely different person once you got married and that if she didn't think she was going to be able to adapt to that, the two of you probably shouldn't be together.

I remember you got really mad at me, because after talking to me, she had pretty well decided to break it off. It took a long time for you to win her back. But it was the right advice.

Back then, I may have not known the fable about the frog and the scorpion, but it's something that's become an important part of the way I've come to see relationships.

The scorpion is stranded on an island after a flood,

and along comes a frog. "Take me to dry land on your back," says the scorpion.

"No," says the frog, "you'll sting me while I'm swimming."

"If I sting you, we'll both drown. Why would I do that?"

So the frog lets the scorpion climb on his back. And they start across the water to land. Just as they reach the deeper water, the frog feels the scorpion's stinger.

"You're stinging me! I'll die, and we'll both drown. Why did you do that?"

"I can't help it," says the scorpion. "I'm a scorpion. That's what I do."

I think we have to recognize people for who they are, even if it's not logical for them to be that way. Even if it's not fair. They are giving you what they've got to give. If you want to be in the relationship, you can accept it or you can go off and pout. Either way, nothing changes. They are who they are.

TERRY: As the son of a coach, whatever was happening when I was growing up seemed normal. For the wife to have to run the family by herself, to be neglected—that seemed normal. From my perspective, it was a burden everyone had to pay. And I guess I got caught up in those assumptions without even knowing I was making them.

BOBBY: A lot of us probably started out a little dishonest about what we expected from marriage. We had the excuse that we didn't know better, that we were too young and too wrapped up in our careers to see what a strain it was going to put on our wives. But ignorance is probably not a good enough excuse for misleading somebody in something so important.

I bet you we could have scared off a lot of women by telling them what was coming—if we knew ourselves.

ROBYN: Look how that same home environment affected Ginger and me. We're ten years apart, the oldest and youngest in the family. But we both ended up modeling our mother. We both have strong characters, but we have both chosen to allow our husbands to be the dominant force in our homes.

I don't think Ginger and I expected anything different. We chose these roles. And we're comfortable in them. But we know most women wouldn't be.

Most of the women I talk to want their husbands home for a certain minimum amount of time. They want a fifty-fifty sharing of responsibilities. That's just inconceivable when your husband is a coach. You had better be ready to pick up a substantial amount of the slack. But I doubt it's any different for wives of politicians or high-powered executives.

GINGER: I bet if you asked the men I work around—and they're mostly men in criminal law—they'd think my husband wears the skirt in our family. They see me as this very aggressive lawyer, operating very comfortably in that man's world. They would die if they saw me at home.

I am exactly like my mother. I do everything. I cook. I clean. I take care of the kids. I take care of my husband.

When we grew up, that was the way Daddy and Mom separated their duties. I don't remember it ever being an issue.

Now, for me, the surprise came when I got married and John came home every day at five P.M. He eats with the kids. He coaches their teams. He reads to them. That was a whole new experience for me. I had to get used to having a husband who wanted to be around the house that much.

When he's not at work, he wants to be with me. I think it's wonderful, but it was a shock.

TERRY: Here's one of the ironies of this whole subject: Hard times might strain your marriage; but good times could be even more of a threat.

When everything is booming, when you're winning and everybody loves you, you can't help feeding off it. "Don't ever leave," people tell you. "We need you too much." And as much as you know about the fickle nature of fans, you revel in the attention.

The awful thing is, that kind of success almost seems to reward you for focusing on your work instead of your family. And if you're not careful, your wife and family begin feeling like you need them less. You may know in your heart that they're the most important things in your life. But all the while, you're organizing your life as if that's not so. The more success you have, the more demands on you. And it can just spiral out of control. That's one reason why I think difficult times might actually pull you closer together as a couple.

Of the four sons in our family, Tommy is the only one who hasn't been divorced. I think Tommy and Linda found great strength together when he was in jobs—like the ones at Duke and Kentucky and the first two years at Auburn—where no matter how hard he worked it was almost impossible to win.

There's no joy in football when you're losing. And the only source of trust, someone who'll stick with you during those times, is your wife. That's when you say, "I can't get by without you," and realize how much you mean it.

TOMMY: There's no doubt my marriage is stronger now than it was nineteen years ago. But, then, I started out different. I think we all do look for our mothers in our wives. The difference with me is that I found someone exactly like my mother.

For the seven years we dated, Linda saw how Mom reacted to things and adjusted. She knew how I was brought up. And she felt comfortable with that.

I believe, too, that a lot of our success has to do with the spiritual commitment we made. There's not only the marriage vows to one another, but also the spiritual commitment to the idea of marriage.

When I was dating Linda, I prayed that she was the one I would marry. In my opinion, a good marriage is not by chance. It's not by luck. It's an answer to prayer.

BOBBY: And boy, it depends so much on the woman.

A young girl marries a doctor and finds out he's going to be on call at four A.M. Or she marries an executive who spends weeks on the road putting together business deals. Military wives sometimes don't see their husbands for months or even years. Being in that kind of relationship requires a certain toughness we don't imagine when we fall in love.

Your mother, it's turned out, is one of the toughest people I've ever known.

You remember that story about Ann back in West Virginia, when some lady who lived back on a country road called to report that some of you boys were trespassing on her property? Well, that woman wanted to give Ann a piece of her mind: "What kind of mother are you to let those boys roam all over creation on other people's land?"

Ol' Ann didn't like to hear someone questioning the job she was doing raising her children, and she demanded, "Where do you live?" Then she jumped in the car and drove on those backcountry West Virginia roads until she made it to this woman's house.

When she got out of the car, this lady was standing on her porch with a rifle in her hands. Now, this is rural West Virginia, and this woman has a gun. That just got Ann going all the more.

"Where is your telephone?" she demanded. "I'm going to call the police on you for threatening me." And she pushed right past that woman on her own porch and went in to use the phone to call the police.

I tell you, Ann ain't afraid of nothin'.

TERRY: This time around I believe I've made the match that will give me the kind of success I want in both my football life and in my family life.

It takes an understanding wife. But I know now that it takes some give on my side, too. I know now that if there's a problem, even if we can't make it go away immediately, we can at least talk about it. Even when I'm absorbed in football, I can show her how important she is to me.

I don't know if I got smarter this time around because of what I've learned about being a more attentive husband or that I was just smart enough to pick the right woman. Shyrl is determined not to lose me to the job, so she does a lot of it with me. She demands that I share my time and attention. Take golf, for instance.

I don't like golf that much, but I've got to play, because it's business. People you need to support your program want you to go out and play golf with them, and they hardly ever ask your wife.

I say, "Well, you've got to have Shyrl play, too." And that throws a lot of these guys. A wife doesn't just go out and play with the men. But Shyrl says, "I'm playing, or you ain't playing." She fights for it. If she thinks I'm doing something in a spare moment that could be hers, she's going to be with me.

I go bird hunting twice a year with some boosters after recruiting's over. She's with me every time. She wanted a shotgun so she could learn how to hunt. Fishing—she's right there with me.

On game days, before the game, she's going to be down on that field, walking around with me until they make her go somewhere else. When we were at Samford, she rode the bus with us.

So I can't take a lot of credit for what holds our marriage together. I hope I've learned from my mistakes. But I still suspect a wife holds it together a lot better than a man. In most coaches' situations, if a wife doesn't hold it together, nobody will.

That's not supposed to be the way it is. But, unfortunately, it is.

8

A Guiding Faith

BOBBY: The older I get, the more confident I've become in the faith I acquired as a child in my parents' home and carried with me all these years. I trust in God's will, even when I don't know what ends are being served.

I can't tell you how many times I've stood at what I thought was a dead end to discover that a door was about to open to a new path, that a new opportunity was about to present itself. If I just believed and trusted enough in Him, the meaning became clear.

STEVE: While you and I might not define spirituality in the same way, Dad, we certainly can agree on its importance in living a truly successful life.

I appreciate the consequences of your faith. I like the peace of mind it's brought you. I envy that. It is not something I have in my own life yet, though I believe I'm working in that direction. Still, we both know, don't we, that the best-lived life is not always peaceful, no matter how much we would like it to be so? Jesus certainly lived in conflict. So did Moses and Muhammad.

I agree with what you often say about the hot fire producing the finest of steel. If there is conflict in our lives, if we do not feel at peace with ourselves or our surroundings, it might be a necessary stage we must work through in order to achieve something satisfying and fulfilling.

BOBBY: But it's my faith that provides something solid to hold on to when everything else is in turmoil.

I've never believed my religious beliefs were a stage I had to pass through. Other parts of my life I had to adjust as I was being tested by my experiences. But my religious faith, the beliefs I acquired as a child, only grew stronger.

You were brought up in those same beliefs. Why can't you find the same comfort in them?

I remember when you made your decision to go to seminary. For years, most of us in the family thought you were headed to med school, that you wanted to become a doctor. Then you decided to switch majors to religion and go on to study for the ministry. I remember being happy for you. I thought you were going to become a preacher.

STEVE: You were happy. Mother, on the other hand, had reservations. She wanted me in the ministry if that's where I belonged. But she wondered if I had really thought it through.

Her concerns bothered me at the time. Mom had endured some frustrating periods during my rebellious years, so I thought she would be pleased. But her reservations turned out to be well-founded.

I transferred from West Virginia to Samford, went on to graduate school, became the pastor of an inner-city church, and got a Ph.D. in philosophy. Much of my pastoral experience was positive. The congregation knew and trusted me. I wasn't some raving radical, but I could do things my way.

At that time, though, my ideas were developing, and I felt less and less comfortable representing an orthodox tradition when I didn't feel orthodox anymore—not unreligious, just not orthodox. I knew I couldn't keep doing that.

The truth is, Dad, I didn't choose theological studies for the express purpose of becoming a "preacher"—at least in the traditional sense. My interests were more personal than professional. I like the church's value system. I was drawn to the idea of people being made whole spiritually. And at the time, seminary and the ministry were the only avenues I knew to pursue those goals. But I was always more motivated by personal enrichment and development than by a "divine calling."

BOBBY: You have always been a searcher, Steve. You need things to be so logical. You need a theory, a theology that connects all the dots. I think sometimes people who burrow so deeply into theology can disappear in the hole they're making. Sometimes they can't accept the easy parts. I think God made it simple. Just accept Him and believe.

STEVE: Actually, I recognize that life is neither logical nor fair. And I'm always suspicious of "the easy parts" of complex ideas.

Now, we're in territory where you and I are not going to be talking the same language. It's where the specifics of our beliefs diverge. You say "God"; I ask, "Whose God? Islam's, Judaism's, Hinduism's?"

If you had been born in India and had been raised in a devoutly Hindu home, you likely would have become a great believer in Hinduism. But regardless of how natural and obvious those Hindu doctrines might have appeared, they wouldn't be true simply because you believed them.

I don't think many Christians would have a problem challenging the "easy facts" of Hinduism, no matter how fervently Hindus believed in them. So why is Christian doctrine obviously true merely because you were raised in a Christian culture and in a devoutly Christian home?

I think we all eventually develop a philosophy of life, an operative faith. And this operative faith can be distilled into some very simple and basic precepts. The Golden Rule is probably one of them. In one form or another, it shows up in most religions and ethical philosophies. The same goes for prohibitions against murder and theft. But all precepts, no matter how simple and basic, must stand up to scrutiny. That's something I demand from anything I'm asked to believe in.

BOBBY: You know, son, this is another one of those situations where it's clear the Bowden family is so much like other families.

Fathers come to me all the time asking me to talk to their sons about their spiritual lives. They are complete strangers, and I can do that. I can talk openly about my faith, witnessing to them in the way I feel led. I do the same with my players, whom I try to treat as if they were my own children.

But when it comes to my real family, my own real children, these topics seem so hard to discuss. Like most fathers, I can sometimes talk about what's deepest in my heart to strangers more easily than to my own children.

STEVE: Well, that's understandable, Dad. I'm a father, too. We all feel we have a special role to play for our children, and it's often the most difficult role of all.

In my case, I probably didn't do much to bridge the communication gap. In graduate school and seminary, I learned the background to the Old and New Testaments. I studied the history and politics of the Gospels. I wanted you to know that the purpose of so many Bible stories wasn't to relate literal history but to serve as lessons, as social and political parables, for potential believers.

I wanted you to know that Adam and Eve weren't historical characters, that the world wasn't made in seven days, that Jonah didn't have to be literally swallowed by a fish for the story to achieve its purpose. Learning about all of that made the old stories live for me in a brand-new way. But it must have sounded like heresy to you.

There was also the context of the times. Those days in the early '70s, all these new ideas were bombarding me from everywhere. The world seemed an enormous stage where dramas of international politics, economics, and morality were playing themselves out. I couldn't understand why so many people couldn't make a connection between the moral and spiritual values they claimed for themselves personally and the need to take a stand on those issues in the larger world. None of the churches I attended as a child, for instance, got involved in the fight to end segregation.

I was thinking about how people who call themselves Christians should be dealing with the war in Vietnam, racism, and the economic disenfranchisement of the poor. And I would come home to a house where the only thing anybody wanted to talk about was football.

BOBBY: Politics have always been the last thing on my mind. I have never taken my religious beliefs as a license to tell other people how to live their lives. I don't believe you can hammer people over the head with your ideas. And I especially don't believe you can do that with young people. They'll turn you off in a flash.

To me, so much of that talk in the '60s and '70s came and went in a gush. Some of what I heard I liked. Some I didn't. But what was left behind for all the people who were asking all those questions and challenging all those ideas was the same old problem: What about your own spiritual life? Have you got yourself personally right with the Lord?

That's my concern. That's my worry for my family, for

my players, for my friends: Have you got yourself personally right with the Lord?

STEVE: That's something I recognize in the tradition we were raised in. One of the defining characteristics of evangelical Protestantism is that no individual is better than any other individual in the eyes of God. Each person must work out his or her own salvation. It's a strictly private and personal affair.

It eventually frustrated me that our religious tradition didn't encourage more active involvement in social issues I thought were natural extensions of the moral life. I don't mean that Christians should prescribe a comprehensive public policy that all persons must follow. I mean that Christians should encourage themselves and others to understand and to get involved in issues outside the church.

What I saw in those days was a kind of Christianity that lacked a social consciousness. It tended to confuse Christian objectives with nationalistic zeal and conservative politics. It rubber-stamped the status quo.

Of course, there's a positive effect of growing up in a tradition more concerned with personal salvation than with social issues. It has separated you, Dad, from that group of professional Christians who are so anxious to tell everybody how to run every detail of their lives.

I'm glad I don't have to turn on my TV and see my father telling people how Christians should vote on everything from books in the public schools to the United States's membership in the United Nations.

BOBBY: Well, that's one thing you don't have to worry about. You're right, my personal faith comes first. And out of my personal faith comes my sense of personal moral obligation. I've got to act on that, because I believe that's what He wants me to do.

That doesn't mean I ram my religion down people's throats. The moral obligation I feel is to help my players become more than just the best football players they can be and more than just the best students they can be. Physical ability will take them so far. An education will take them so far. But there will come a time in their lives when they need more than that. And I want these young men to know there's something available to them, something they can make their own in a way that satisfies their own spiritual needs.

Since I've been a head coach, I've always gotten the team together at the beginning of the season to visit a church. These days, I pick two churches. One Sunday, we go to a predominantly black church; on the next, we go to a predominantly white one. Every year we go to different churches and almost never to the one I belong to.

When these players first come to Florida State, I write every parent, telling them I'm going to take their sons to church on two Sundays before the season. I tell them we're going to have prayer before ball games and sometimes on the field. I tell them we might read from the Bible or from religious articles. And if they don't want me to, I tell the parents, I won't include their boys in any of that.

I've been doing that all these years, and I've only had two parents ask me to leave their sons out. One was a

Muslim family. And the other was a Southern Baptist family whose mother believed that her boy shouldn't go to any other church but their own.

I think most parents want this kind of environment for their kids, even if they don't go to church themselves. I know it's important to many of them, because every year I have players and parents tell me that's one of the reasons they chose our program. It gives these kids an anchor, something to hold on to as they begin to shape their adult lives. It's a moral base.

STEVE: We might disagree on the motivation for developing that sense of moral obligation, Dad. But here's where our religious sensibilities intersect. I'm as rabid a believer in doing the right thing as I was when I was a fifteen-year-old.

I think there are pretty good reasons to practice the virtues of integrity, honesty, and trustworthiness. I believe you should care for others when there's nothing in it for you. I believe you should be doing all those things—but not because I'm afraid there's a supernatural being that will disapprove or punish you. That's not my motivation. It just seems clear to me that we would all rather live in a virtuous society than in a virtueless society.

I hope there is a personal God out there. The way I figure it, if the cosmos is ultimately organized that way and I'm living the best life I can, then I'm in pretty good shape.

BOBBY: In football, we talk about "overcoaching" a game, interfering with the flow more than you need to.

You end up confusing the players, and you risk messing up your chances to win.

I think you're overcoaching your spirituality. You're needlessly overcomplicating the game plan.

STEVE: I know that you can become so open-minded your brains fall out. But closed-mindedness isn't the proper response to the danger. There's nothing wrong with questioning what others accept as gospel. If beliefs have merit, they'll stand up under intense scrutiny.

You know where I got my first lessons in questioning things? Mom. Despite all our battles, she's the one who encouraged me to think for myself, to not let other people do my thinking for me.

Mom spent a lot of time in our early years helping us with reading and writing. She always made sure there were books around. When I got to seminary, not only was I fascinated at everything there was to learn, I was also willing to question anything and everything, to separate the wheat from the chaff.

I wanted theory to grow out of facts instead of having the facts arranged to satisfy a theory. It was a natural outgrowth of my personality—and Mom's influence. And it makes sense. It's one of the things I'm most grateful for growing up in our home.

BOBBY: What I think is interesting is how the more you've read and the more you've experienced, the more you're led to question the faith you were brought up with. It's been just the opposite with me.

The more I've experienced, the more challenges thrown at me, the greater my confidence in the things I believe. What I don't understand just increases my awe of the breadth of His power. It doesn't threaten my faith, it strengthens it. I guess it's that old question about whether you see the glass of water half full or half empty. I tend to see it half full.

I would love for you to share what I have. It requires a leap of faith, I know. But the rewards are plentiful. For me, one of them is in not having to question what I don't entirely understand.

I get letters all the time from former players thanking me for something I said or wrote or read to them. Sometimes, I can't even remember what it was. But it somehow stuck with them and made a difference in their lives. I've seen people change their lives around, becoming entirely new human beings through faith. I call that a miracle, and it's the only proof I need of God working in our lives.

It worked for Mark Bonasorte, who was a defensive back on four of my first teams at Florida State, including that '79 squad that went undefeated in the regular season. In 1995, Mark was inducted into the Florida State Hall of Fame. But he had to turn around his life to get there.

After he finished his playing career, Mark went to Jacksonville, got into business and somehow got mixed up in drugs. He was arrested and had to spend some time in jail. He worked his way out of that and now has a successful life and a wonderful family.

When he was inducted into our Hall of Fame, it was on a Friday night during the '95 season. I always spend the nights before games with the team. But Mark said he really wanted me to be at the ceremony, so I went. What he wanted me to hear was a letter I had written him years ago when he got in trouble.

The letter was about making mistakes in life. I wrote him that everybody makes mistakes, that some people get caught, some don't. The important thing to remember, I said, was that you can't accept that as being the end. You may have to pay a price for what you've done, but it doesn't mean you're a failure. You can get beyond it if you have faith.

I didn't remember any of that until Mark read it out. Over forty years, I'm sure I said similar things or wrote similar letters to other players. Those are things I believe with all my heart. But you never know if they're listening. For Mark, the words came at a time when he needed to know that he wasn't alone. I wasn't preaching. But I was helping him spiritually without even knowing it.

That's how God works in our lives when we give Him a chance.

STEVE: We both make leaps of faith, Dad. We just jump off at different points.

I'm not a pessimist. I see the half-full glass, too. But what will ultimately console me in my spiritual life is a philosophy that encompasses a broad range of questions about who we are and how we should behave toward one another.

I like your example of Mark Bonasorte. You gave him good advice. Our beliefs should allow us to recognize that losing is not the same as final defeat; nor is winning the same as ultimate victory. Isn't that what you mean when you say "Winning's only part of the game"?

To find the kind of success we really want, we must

live as true to our beliefs as we know how. To that end, Dad, your example is as worth emulating as it ever was.

There are lots of paths to the same destination. Maybe a sincere commitment to the journey is the crucial part.

BOBBY: Sincerity is important. But where we differ, Steve, is that I still believe in a specific path.

I am a Christian, because I choose to be a Christian. I believe that only through the Holy Bible and through the acceptance of Christ as our personal savior can we receive the blessings of eternal life and the joy God promises.

I am not going to impose that belief on anyone. Not on my players. Not even on you. But it is at the core of my spiritual life. Without that faith, I can't be the person, the coach, the husband, and the father I want to be.

Part II

LESSONS OF THE GAME

9

THE LESSONS OF FOOTBALL

BOBBY: I bet you every coach at every level of sports has stood in front of players at one time or another and talked about the lessons you learn on courts and fields that you can take with you the rest of your life. That's because, for those of us who've spent our lives in sports, the lessons couldn't be more clear.

What teaches the value of teamwork, self-discipline, and perseverance more effectively?

STEVE: This is something I've been thinking about lately, Dad. Someone who knows my background asked me what I got out of playing football. The more I thought about it, the smaller my list got.

There is certainly the pleasure of playing itself, the fun of competing at that particular time and in that particular place. That's a worthwhile experience. But when it comes to enduring lessons, there aren't many that I would attribute directly or exclusively to football.

The most unique and lasting value I derived directly from football was the experience of pushing beyond my physical limits. In my case, I also learned the meaning of the word *determination*. But that's about it. Everything else I either took with me into football or learned elsewhere.

Football can certainly teach the positive values of discipline, teamwork, perseverance, and patience. Some players find themselves challenged in ways they were never challenged before. Others are required to achieve levels of discipline and determination never asked of them before. And still others may learn the lessons of effective teamwork.

But those same values are taught in just about any setting—in business, in the classroom, in marriage—where there are goals to be achieved and ends to be realized. Those who learn them have a good chance to succeed. Those who don't will struggle.

In most regards, athletes are in no better or worse positions than anyone else. The student who wants to make all A's must work harder than the average student. Same for the factory line worker who wants to be foreman. Same for the aspiring small businessman who wants to grow his business. In each case, those who practice the virtues of discipline, perseverance, and hard work have the best chance to succeed—whether they acquired those virtues on an athletic field or in the Future Farmers of America.

Dad, you're one of the best coaches a player could ever hope to play for. Your lifestyle and beliefs have influenced an untold number of athletes. I would credit you—and the staff you direct—for all those positive influences on players' lives. But I wouldn't credit the sport itself.

Some very successful players seemed to have learned important lessons about life from football. Others, equally successful, seem to have mastered nothing they can apply off the field. So I'm reluctant to correlate football success with personal success, or football skill with personal virtue.

BOBBY: I think you're right that people who are paying attention can pick up the important lessons of life doing just about whatever they set their hearts to. But they have to make that commitment, and they've got to be willing to test themselves in some way that will demonstrate whether they're succeeding or not. Sports require you to commit, and they tell you immediately whether you're measuring up.

You try to play football without having your heart in it, and you'll end up on your butt pretty dadgum quick.

Want to know how you're doing? Look at the score.

Let's be honest now, sports are not life. In real life, there ain't no official blowing a whistle on you when you step out of bounds or when you cross over the line of scrimmage too soon. There's no clock. And there's no one counting to make sure the sides are even all the time. Sometimes, in fact, in life outside of sports it seems there are no rules at all.

So maybe what most of us need, especially when we're growing up, is a place where we can practice playing by rules we can all agree on, where we can get a clear idea of where we stand in relationship to others who're playing, and where we get to hear a few cheers when we're playing hard. That stuff is doggone hard to come by outside of athletics.

Now, let's talk about football in particular. One of the things I like about it is that it's complicated. If we say sports are not really like life because life is so much more complicated, then maybe football is a step or two closer to real life because of the complexity built into the game.

First of all, there are the numbers. There are eleven people on each side. And since we separate specialties into defense, offense, punting, and place-kicking, there are twenty-three or twenty-four separate jobs. To play a game on Saturday afternoon, we may use forty-five or fifty kids, subbing for injured players and giving a breather to first-teamers. To practice for a game, we need a hundred or more. So when you hear football coaches talking as if they're commanding an army getting ready for battle, it ain't much of an exaggeration.

Now with so many people to organize, with so much potential for things to go wrong, football demands an enormous amount of organization. We break teams down into segments, like departments in a corporation. There's an assistant coach for each segment, like a department manager. For a game plan to work, for the whole team to have success, each segment and each player in the segment have to understand the plan and execute it.

You see where I'm going? The kind of experience you get working in a system like this can serve you pretty well in whatever organization you end up working in.

Of course, you have to pay attention, just as you say, Steve. But if you ain't paying attention on my team, you ain't playing. And that's a pretty good lesson in and of itself. There are plenty of organizations you can join that will let you hang around whether or not you make much effort to contribute. The thing about team sports is that you have to fulfill your responsibility for the team to advance. And a lot of times you have to do that when you can't see the immediate purpose of your job.

That All-American tackle down there on the offensive line may not get a glimpse of the ball the whole game. He may not see much more than belly buttons and size 14 football cleats for sixty minutes. But you better believe he's crucial to the execution of every play.

Every receiver has to run convincing routes, whether the ball is thrown to them or not; otherwise, the defense doubles up on your other guys, and you can forget about the passing game. Quarterbacks and running backs have to make great fakes to give plays a chance to unfold. We need everybody blocking.

Think of what we required from ol' Edgar Bennett when he was our fullback. When I saw Edgar play in high school, I knew he was someone who could play for anybody and at just about any position that required catching or running with the ball—wide receiver, tailback, fullback. Well, he ended up playing fullback in the same backfield with guys like Amp Lee, who were both smaller and more the classic tailbacks in style.

Because we pass so much using three or more receivers, the fullback is not in the game nearly as much as he would be if we were a running team. And when he is in there, we're asking him to block a lot. Can you imagine how frustrating that must be for someone with Edgar's talent? He can look in the paper every Sunday and see running backs all over the nation getting all those carries, and here he is splitting playing time with a tailback and a bunch of receivers.

By the time Edgar was a junior, it was clear this was a guy who was going to play in the NFL, and people were starting to buzz in his ear about coming out for the draft early. It happens every year with the good juniors. But it had to be a special kind of temptation for Edgar, who knew he could be running with the best backs in the country.

When I talked to him after his junior season, I told him what I tell all my players: Hang in there for your senior year. Get your degree. Get another year of experience and muscle. It will only make you better and more valuable to the pros.

Well, Edgar decided to stay for his senior year in 1991. We tried to get him the ball as much as we could that year, but Amp was having a great season, too. And we had Casey Weldon passing for a bunch of yards. Once again Edgar had to split time with a lot of others, and I'm sure he questioned his decision a couple of times. But he was drafted by the Green Bay Packers and helped that team's resurgence. He's a millionaire player now, and there ain't anybody who follows football who doesn't know how good Edgar Bennett is.

I believe he knows he helped himself by doing exactly what he did at Florida State. He showed tremendous patience and dedication while people all around him were saying "Take the money." Now, he's got it all. But he couldn't know how it was going to turn out. He just trusted in his teammates and in his coaches, who were preaching every day: Take responsibility. Do your job the best you know how. And you will succeed.

I think that's pretty good advice for anybody. And if I were a corporate manager, I wouldn't mind a bit getting employees who came to me already schooled in those lessons—whether they came from playing football or from the Future Farmers of America. I just think the lessons are a little easier to learn on the football field.

TERRY: I want to go back to something Steve said about pushing beyond your physical limits. Even if that's the only lesson of football you walk away with, it's a pretty good one.

For people who've never played competitive sports, the idea of "playing with pain" is a touchy subject. It's difficult to talk about unless you're very precise about what you mean. But it's amazing to me how important it is to learn to play football with pain—to have an arm that's so sore you think it's broken, but you go ahead and play anyway. Or to think your teammates are depending on you so much, you play with a finger that's bent back and crooked and maybe dislocated. I just think that's one of the greatest lessons you learn.

Here's its value: When a young man becomes older and he doesn't feel so well and he's got a family to feed, he will get up and go to work. Or when the company is depending on him to be somewhere at a certain time, he's going to be there even if he's hurting. That's because he's learned something about putting aside his own discomfort for something he values, for a responsibility he has to someone else.

BOBBY: You know I agree with you, but this is a topic that's easy to misunderstand. Coaches face criticism all the time about the violence of football, about the risks we expose our players to.

TERRY: People who aren't familiar with the game will say, "You're risking the health of players because you want to win at all costs."

From a coach's standpoint, though, risking injury is the last thing you want. You can't win by getting people injured or by playing people who are seriously hurt.

If you play someone who's injured, not only are you risking losing him for an even longer period, you're weakening the position he plays—you're weakening your whole offense or defense—by having him in there. So injuries are the enemy. You do everything you can to avoid them.

I've got two full-time trainers and two full-time doctors traveling with my team. There's at least one doctor on the field at all times. Anytime a guy falls down I have people all over him. Because of what we know about avoiding injuries and rehabilitating them, catastrophic injuries are rare. But that doesn't mean muscles aren't going to be strained and bruised, bones aren't going to be broken, and ligaments aren't going to be torn.

Though it sounds awful, the truth is, no one ever died of a broken finger or from getting a couple of teeth knocked out. And I believe the lessons you learn tolerating the pain, overcoming the fears of injury, and pushing yourself to come back from injuries—those are lessons you take with you the rest of your life.

It hurts to train for a marathon. It hurts to swim one more lap when your body is screaming for you to quit. It hurts to move the weight for one more rep. But that's exactly the kind of effort that makes you stronger, that makes you better.

I always tell my players, "Men, your object is to push yourself to that point where you can't go any farther and then allow us to push you farther—without balking, without walking off or cussing or turning your back to the coach."

They must take themselves to that limit that all human beings have, then for them to get better, they have to let us push them farther.

BOBBY: And for them to put themselves in that position, they must trust us and they must trust their teammates.

That's a word you don't hear very often in explanations of lessons you take away from football, but I think it's an important one. Trust may be the toughest thing to ask from another human being. You're asking them to put themselves at risk with the promise that you won't let them down.

Trust is the absolute last thing a lot of kids are willing to invest these days. For many of the ones we see, there's nothing in their experience that suggests much of a payoff in trusting somebody else. The lessons they come to school with are lessons of the street: Get the other guy before he gets you. Never turn your back. Don't depend on anybody.

Raw talent creates stars of some of these kids. They

are so good in high school they seem like men among boys. They don't have to fit into a team. Some coaches will fit a team around them. They're too good not to play.

Then they come to us. They show up in August and stand on that field for the first time with fifteen, eighteen, twenty other freshmen who were stars back home, too. Ahead of them on the team are sixty other guys who were also high school stars and who are now older, smarter, bigger, and faster. Suddenly, these kids are among peers. Or even more likely, they are facing competition, for the first time in their lives, that will force them to improve their skills or stay on the sidelines. And for them to get better, they have to learn to trust.

I still think about my freshman year at the University of Alabama, when it was my turn to run out on a practice field with all those other scholarship players. I looked around and thought, "I ain't never going to work my way into this lineup." I got so homesick, I transferred to Samford without ever really giving it a shot. That's something I regret to this day. That was almost fifty years ago and I remember it like it was yesterday. It was my decision to leave. It was my responsibility. But I remember, too, that nobody took me aside and encouraged me to hang in there. Nobody said they knew how I was feeling and that I just had to trust the coaches and trust my own talent.

So when I became a head coach I decided to make sure my young players and their parents know I understand what they're going through. I write the parents of all the freshmen. I tell them I know how homesick they'll be, how they feel they'll never get a chance to play, and how they wish they were somewhere else. Trust in us, I say. We wouldn't have offered that kid a scholarship if we didn't think he was going to play for us.

Have patience. It's one of the first lessons you have to learn, I tell them. Then I remind them about Charlie Ward.

We offered Charlie a scholarship out of high school, but his test scores weren't quite high enough for him to be a full qualifier. Instead of going to some other school or attending Florida State for a year without having a chance to practice and play, Charlie stayed out and studied until he made his score. Then, for three years, he waited his turn behind three other quarterbacks.

Here was a guy who was going to become one of the most honored players in the history of college football. He was an All–American and Florida State's first Heisman Trophy winner. He led us to our first national championship. Yet he set on the bench for three years.

Charlie never complained a minute. He did whatever we asked, played whatever role we needed. Then, when it became his turn, he stepped on the field, and from that moment on there was never a question who the leader of that team was.

I wish we could claim that Charlie learned how to be Charlie at Florida State. But he came to us that way. He's the son of a coach and a teacher. By high school, Charlie had already learned what sports can teach you about patience and determination.

Now, when young players sulk and insist they're too

good to be sitting on the bench waiting their turn to start, I can point them to the locker where we hang Charlie Ward's retired jersey:

"Would you say you're better than No. 17?"

10

VIOLENCE AND DISCIPLINE

TERRY: As long as we're talking about lessons coaches require, we might as well take on another controversial issue: aggression.

I think you have to teach aggression. You have to continually work on bringing out aggression, on making athletes play fiercely—or as the old cliché goes, with "reckless abandon." And you create that by the way in which you practice, by habitually driving a kid to go full-speed in drills, flinging his body around the field.

In the old days, I think coaches even encouraged fighting. I don't think it's the worst thing in the world that players get so caught up in the emotion that they go at one another from time to time. But we stop the fights, because we don't want them building habits that can lose us a ball game.

A fight in a game can get players ejected. It almost

always ends in a penalty that stops a drive or gives the other guys a first down. So we preach something that seems impossible: We want our athletes playing with "reckless abandon" and, at the same time, "under control." How do you manage to do that? By knowing where you are in the game and what's appropriate, what's expected, under those circumstances.

BOBBY: Here we are again, son, running head-on into territory that creates so much misunderstanding. There is no doubt that football, probably more than any other sport, requires a high level of physical aggressiveness. You can't play without it. But we live in a time where the violence all around us—in the streets, in the schools—scares us so much that it's hard for a lot of people to separate talk of aggression in a game from the reality of violent aggression outside of sports.

When I came along as a player and as a young coach, there used to be fights in practice all the time. Anytime people are involved in a sport where physical contact is a crucial part of the game, fights are liable to break out. Of course, if players have pads and helmets on, the ones most likely to get hurt are the ones who try to hit with their bare hands. So fights usually turn into wrestling matches that are so exhausting that pretty soon both players' tongues are hanging out. After practice I make the players come over to me and convince me whatever set them off is over, that they'll walk off the field as teammates.

Learning self-control is crucial in a game where you can lose everything because of a fight on the field. And as young men, learning how to walk away from confrontations is a survival skill they'd better learn to master before they're out in the world.

One of my favorite examples is William Floyd, the great fullback we had who went on to win a Super Bowl ring with the San Francisco 49ers. He was a great kid and so tough that everybody knew not to mess with him. But sometimes his temper got the best of him.

When William was a freshman, he got into it with Dan Footman in practice. Now, think about these two guys, two of the toughest players we've ever had, both bound for careers in the NFL. Floyd is this big kid—maybe six-one or six-two and 220 pounds—a terrifically talented fullback who is just learning how to play in our offense. But Dan is a man, a giant of a defensive end—six-seven and something like 275 pounds—who is fighting his way back after an operation and a full year of rehabilitation.

A lot of people thought Dan would never play again. But he worked so hard for that year he had to take off, that he came back strong and fast. And as far as he is concerned, his whole life, his shot at a career in the pros, depends on that knee holding up. Then along comes this smart-aleck freshman, blocking in a drill where he's not supposed to hit anybody below the waist, and he tries to cut Footman's legs out from under him.

Well, Footman was on Floyd in a second. And he would have killed him. Yet Floyd, despite being in the wrong to start with and despite being younger and outmatched in size and strength, comes right back at him. That's William. If you challenge him, he's going to come at you with everything he's got.

Well, somehow we were able to get them apart. But

we had a devil of a time keeping William from starting it up all over again. As far as he was concerned it wasn't over until he faced old Dan down. And Dan wasn't about to let this kid do that.

So I called William into my office. "What you've got to do," I told him, "is walk away from those kinds of fights." Which, of course, is the last thing in the world someone with William Floyd's pride wants to hear.

He comes right back with, "I ain't never backed down from nobody. I ain't scared of nobody." All that sort of thing.

Now, you want someone with William's kind of pride and determination on your team. I loved his spirit. That same year, at LSU, William saved a sure two points by making one of the most incredible plays I've ever seen.

The weather in Baton Rouge is awful. It's raining, and there's mud everywhere. We're fighting for every yard, and finally, after three quarters, we're winning. But we run into trouble trying to kick an extra point after a touchdown. The ball slips out of the holder's hand. And instead of taking the blocked kick, he tries to find somebody to throw to into the end zone.

Well, an LSU defensive back intercepts the doggone thing and is off and running the opposite way without a Florida State player in sight.

If he scores, it's only worth 2 points. And we're ahead by 11. But we've got almost a whole quarter left to play on LSU's home field in the pouring rain. And the last thing we need is for that team to get all fired up after a 100-yard interception.

On the game film, you see this speedy little defensive back running untouched for 90 yards. Then, out of nowhere comes old William, who had been blocking on the opposite side of the line for the extra point. He gives the guy maybe a 20-yard head start, sprints the length of the field and catches him from behind on the 10.

So what could have been an inspiration for the other guys gets turned inside out and becomes a rallying point for us. They don't score again, and we win one of our toughest games of that season. That's what William Floyd's pride can accomplish when it's pointed in the right direction. But that fight in practice with Footman and William's inability to let it rest showed the trouble he could get himself into if he couldn't control himself.

"You've got to learn to walk away from this kind of thing," I told him again. "You've got to learn to back off, son. I don't care how tough you are or how strong you are, all a little ol' 120-pound guy has to do is pull out a gun and pull the trigger, and you're nobody."

William, like a lot of our kids, grew up in a neighborhood where you're measured by your refusal to back down from anybody. But a lot of those kids who stay in that environment don't survive. And nobody who is determined to solve every disagreement with violence is going to make it long in the world outside those neighborhoods. It was very tough for William. But he's a bright kid. As football put him more and more in the spotlight, he learned that he would have to handle himself differently. So, gradually, he figured out how to walk away from some fights.

That temper will always be there. But I like to think that William found a way to use football to channel his aggression. That's how I explain the value of football to people who think we're training players to be violent people. It's the other way around, I say. We're taking people, some of whom might be very violent, and we're giving them an outlet for that aggression. It's a way to get it out of their system.

When our kids come off the field, they ain't got nothing left to go out and pick a fight. They know what I'm going to say if I hear one of them goes out and gets in trouble. I say, "Maybe I ain't working y'all hard enough. If you have enough energy to be running around all night, maybe we ought to be running a few more wind sprints after practice."

TERRY: I don't want anybody to misunderstand. The kind of aggressiveness you need to play football obviously is not appropriate off the field. In fact, I don't think a football level of aggressiveness is much help anywhere but on a football field—or maybe on a battlefield.

I know there are lots of critics of football who believe one of the lessons players take away from the game is that you can always get your way if you're physically aggressive enough. But it's just not true.

BOBBY: In fact, even football teaches the value of controlling yourself. We design offensive plays to attack defenses that are overly aggressive. We run reverses and screens that just take the heart right out of defenses that are so fired up they forget where they are on the field.

I love it when I see guys on the other side so worked up they're pawing the ground to get at us. I've scored a lot of touchdowns on those kinds of teams.

You just ain't gonna win at anything playing out of control.

TERRY: And even the under-control aggression is something you save just for competition. When I hear of studies that argue that male athletes are involved in a disproportionate number of violent assaults and date rapes, it bothers me. If that's true—and I would have to look closely at a study like that—the reasons may have less to do with what sports teach than with what society allows privileged people to get away with.

A guy recruited to play football at schools like Florida State or Auburn is among the best athletes in the country. Chances are, he's been given preferential treatment all his life, told how special he was and how rules that applied to others didn't necessarily hold for him. As a result, a lot of these kids aren't clear about what's acceptable behavior and what's not. Everything was okay no matter what they did. So if we want them to start acting differently once they get to college and throughout the rest of their lives, then we've got to explain the rules, and we've got to enforce them consistently.

BOBBY: That gets us to the hard part. What do you do when the player fails to understand those rules or maybe even understands them and still can't control himself?

You've got a kid who gets in a fight in a bar. Or someone pulls a gun at a party. Or you've got a situation like the one Coach Tom Osborne had at Nebraska during the '95 season.

Tom had a star tailback who gets arrested for assaulting a former girlfriend. It's all over the papers and on TV just about every day, because Nebraska is undefeated and heading to the national championship game at the Fiesta Bowl.

Tom suspends the player for a few games, but lets him play in the last couple, including the bowl game. And the columnists are teeing off on him: "How can you let this criminal stay on your football team after what he's done? What kind of message does that send?"

I talked to Tom a couple of times during the season and I know what he was going through. I was in complete sympathy, even though I didn't know the specifics of the case. Here's what I tell people:

Nothing is as cut-and-dried as we try to make it out to be. I'm a great believer in looking at each case individually. I can't sit in Tallahassee and tell somebody in California or Nebraska what they ought to do when a player gets in trouble. But I think there ought to be some logic in the process.

We have a whole system of criminal justice—police, lawyers, courts, counselors, jails, all of that. So let's let those folks all do their jobs and see what happens.

Then we've got the regulations of the university. Well, let's apply the same rules to players that apply to all students and see what happens.

If the criminal system says "Guilty!" and locks my player up, so be it. If the university says we're not going to have any student acting that way and kicks him out, so be it. My problem comes when all these authorities with all their experts decide that the kid can walk the streets and can be in school, and then they pass the buck to me to decide whether or not he can play football.

Well, if you give me that authority, I'm going to exercise it. You've already decided what's good for society and good for the school. Now, I'm going to make my decision based on what I think is good for the player and good for the team. I'm going to look for the right balance.

TERRY: A lot of people think it's tough for a coach to kick a guy off the team, especially if he's a really good player. But, if you ask me, that's the easiest thing to do if you're thinking only about your own career.

It makes most of the alumni happy. Reporters write it up. You get a lot of credit for being a strict disciplinarian, for putting the team and school above any individual player—when most of the time you know you'll survive whether you have this particular kid or not. Nebraska won every game without that tailback and could have won the Fiesta Bowl without him, too.

But if you're really determined to be the kind of leader of young men you claim to be, you have to keep something else in mind. You look at these players, and the last thing you think is *kid*. Some of them weigh three hundred pounds. They stand six-seven or six-eight. But these are kids. Many are younger even than their ages. And for many of them, about the only thing that's consistently working in their lives is football.

So when one of them gets in trouble and you have choices to make, part of the decision—the part you usually can't tell people about—is how badly that young man might need to keep connected with the team during a difficult time. Maybe his mother is dead. Maybe his father is in jail for drugs. If you turn him loose, what are his chances of making it on his own?

The thing is, though, you can't put all that stuff out there for a reporter to write about. You have to protect the player's privacy. You have to protect his family.

Even if you are able to make that argument, people won't buy it. They are so ready to believe that winning is the only thing you care about, they'll never accept that you're thinking about the kid's best interest.

Isn't it funny that the whole country seems to want coaches to treat their players as more than just athletes, to treat them like their own children, then when you behave like a father all you hear is, "He's trying to win at all costs"?

BOBBY: When I have a kid who gets in trouble, I try to leave him some thread of hope. If we're so big on using football to teach the lessons of life, don't we have to offer these kids hope that there's a way to fight their way back after they stumble and fall? That even if they make mistakes they will still have a chance to succeed? Sometimes players do something so disruptive or dangerous you have to let them go. But if there's still a chance I can have an influence on a player in trouble, I hate to cut the string between us. If something were to happen to him afterward, I would feel so much to blame.

That's what separates a coach from a professor. If you're a professor, and a student leaves your class at three o'clock, that's the last you'll hear of him until the next class. If the kid goes out and commits murder, nobody would ever think of calling you up and asking what went wrong, why can't you control your students? There wouldn't be any editorials about how ashamed the English department should be for having somebody like that enrolled in literature classes.

But a coach is held responsible for all his players every minute. We do get those calls. People do write those editorials.

I made up my mind a long time ago not to make decisions based on public opinion. I never wanted fans or the press or anybody telling me how to discipline my players.

I try to treat these players as I would my own children. People write me critical letters saying how a kid is "a disgrace to the team" and that I ought to kick him off. I write back and ask, "What if he were your son? What would you want me to do then?"

And usually I don't get a letter back.

II

Kids These Days

TERRY: It's tough enough to balance our concern for players' well-being with the need to enforce rules when we agree with the rules. It's even harder when the ax comes down on kids for things that don't seem much of a threat to society or to higher education.

For instance, it seems like every time I'm on one of those radio call-in shows, I have to reassure fans for the umpteenth time that I won't allow my players to dance and point and taunt on the field. Fans get hot, because that kind of stuff, by their way of thinking, doesn't show class. To them, it indicates disrespect for the game and the school.

Well, I guess I come from a similar background as most of our fans. I don't think that kind of behavior shows class either. But I don't buy the fact that players don't respect the game the way they did in the old days.

And it makes me feel a little hypocritical coming down on the players for the antics they grew up with. So many people seem to want the young people of the '90s to play the game in the style of the '50s and '60s.

When I was playing football for you, Dad, and was lucky enough to score a touchdown—which, of course, was always in a scrimmage, since you would never put me in a game—I didn't point. I didn't dance. I didn't taunt. I handed the ball back to the official and ran to the huddle for the extra point. But after the game, as soon as I got outside the locker room, I would reach into my back pocket for my tobacco can and grab "a pinch to put between my cheek and gum."

That's because my hero at the time was Walt Garrison, the Dallas Cowboys running back. Walt Garrison didn't taunt or dance. And he always handed the ball right back to the official after he scored. But he did do commercials for chewing tobacco. And I wanted to be just like Walt Garrison, because he played on Sundays.

My players today are not chewing tobacco, which is a whole lot worse for you than dancing in the end zone. But they are trying to be like their heroes, the ones they see on Sundays in the NFL. And those guys do point and dance. They "shoot their guns" at opposing players and rip off their helmets after good plays. And our kids are copying them, just like we copied our heroes. But inside, the college players of today are no different than when you or I were playing. Am I wasting my time trying to get people to understand that?

BOBBY: I don't really know how to answer that, although you know I tend to be a little more forgiving of my players than all you ultraconservatives up there in Alabama.

No doubt about it, when I was in school and when you played for me at West Virginia, we didn't show emotion when we did something on the football field. But the fact is, that's become a part of today's football. Our kids get it from the pros. They watch NFL players dance and celebrate on Sundays. They see the crowd go crazy. And they want to do the same thing on Saturdays.

I think the whole thing started with Muhammad Ali in the '60s. He was the first to stand up and say, *I, me, my . . . I am the greatest. I am the prettiest.* Back when we were coming up, it was always *we, us, our.* It had to be *team.* Then, along comes this great athlete who says all these things—and backs it all up. But if you can do everything you say, then it ain't bragging, is it?

Your story about copying Walt Garrison reminds me of my own football days in Birmingham. We didn't have television, but my high school coaches chewed tobacco. So did my college coaches. Anytime you were around them, you had to be ready to jump out of the way real quick. You could smell the aroma of Red Man or Beechnut in the huddle. So when I started coaching, the first thing I had to do was go buy me some chewing tobacco to be like my old coaches. And though I know I shouldn't, I still chew from time to time.

I shouldn't say this, but I've always felt everybody's got to have something they do that's at least a little bad. I try not to use profanity. I don't drink or smoke. I don't chase women. So I guess my bad is a little chew every now and then. Your mother nearly has a fit, so I have to choose my places. But I guess if that's the worst thing I do, she and other folks can forgive me.

It's the same way with the kids, who have come by their bad habits the same way I did—by imitating people they respect. If dancing and pointing fingers when they're excited about playing football is the worse thing they do, I reckon we can forgive them.

JEFF: I'm very sympathetic with the players on this one. Football is a game. And within certain obvious limitations, the players have a right to have a little fun.

At this level, football is already tough on these kids. We place so many demands on their bodies and on their minds. We're on 'em every day: "You've got to step into this gap on this play . . . You have to hit with this shoulder . . . You'd better wrap your arms on this tackle."

So the kid practices this all week. He's worked his butt off to get ready, and here comes the play we've been working on. He makes his read. He steps into that gap. He hits with the right shoulder. He wraps his arms. And he makes a big play.

He's so excited, so pumped that he did everything right, he jumps up with his hands in the air and does a little dance. And we're telling him he can't do this?

I think it's ridiculous.

BOBBY: The Florida State player everybody thinks of when they talk about the end zone prancing is Deion Sanders. And he's a pretty good example of how people misread a player's style as some indication of disrespect for the game. I don't think I've ever had a player who had more love or respect for football than Deion. And I can't think of many who were more admired by coaches and teammates.

Around the players, Deion never played the star. That was for public consumption. His last season, he wasn't even on scholarship. He paid his own way, because, by that time, he was playing minor league baseball for the New York Yankees.

Before he turned pro as a baseball player, we would excuse him from spring practice so he could play baseball for Florida State. Now, if you let most players out of practice, they'll stay as far away from those drills and those hot practice fields as they can. But Deion was different. On days the baseball team wasn't practicing or playing in a game, he would put on the pads and come out and practice with us. That's how crazy he was. And the players just ate it up.

I've had great players who would do just about anything they could to avoid practicing. But Deion never asked out of anything. He was a great practice player, going hard on every play.

Come Saturdays, of course, Deion was going to put on a show. That was before the taunting rules. And I figured I could let him do his dancing as long as we weren't drawing any penalties and it wasn't holding up the game. That was his style. And not only did he thrive on it, he could get our whole team going. As long as he wasn't breaking any rules I wasn't about to do anything to take away from the enthusiasm on our team.

Nowadays, of course, they'd come up with a whole set of rules aimed just at Deion.

TERRY: In fact, we're in a period right now where there's an obsession with eliminating show-off behavior by penalizing every act on the field. And I'm thinking to myself, who are the people making these rules?

Are they the contemporaries of these athletes or are they people who long for the day when it was one-platoon football? Back when everyone came from the same neighborhood because they only gave scholarships to one group of people?

As much as we tend to avoid the subject, a lot of this discussion is about race. Not so long ago in college football, cultural diversity meant you were either a city white kid or a country white kid. Over the last twenty years we have done a good thing by cutting across cultural and racial lines in athletics. In fact, we're probably doing a better job of that than most other institutions. When we run our teams out there on Saturdays now, the ratio of black players to white players is much higher than the ratio of black students to white students in our universities.

But the people who run college football and those who buy tickets and contribute to booster funds are not much different than in an earlier era. They are mostly middle-aged white people. And many of them insist on seeing football played in exactly the way they remember twenty or thirty years ago. Those are the people making the rules. And they are the people for whom the rules are made.

BOBBY: I've always tried to appreciate both sides of this argument. I come from that older, conservative generation myself. But being around these youngsters has put me pretty much on their side.

One of the bad things about being in the majority all your life, of associating almost exclusively with people who are just like you, is that you don't have to second-guess yourself much. If everything you know is white, white, white, you can convince yourself pretty easily that race is never a factor in anything.

I hear people say that all the time: "This isn't about race. This is just about football." Or, "This isn't about race, it's just about common sense."

But your view changes when you work closely with these black young men. You come to see things from their point of view. What's common sense to them may be something entirely different, including the feeling that, often, it *is* about race.

The overwhelming number of our players are black athletes. Most of the coaches these kids have been exposed to, at least on the college level, are white. Almost all of their professors are white. Almost all of the students on our campus—90 percent of some thirty thousand students—are white. Now, for us as white people to insist that we understand where these black kids are coming from, what they're going through—well, that requires some assumptions I don't think we have a right to make.

We're pretty quick to argue that you shouldn't judge somebody before you walk a mile in their shoes. Well, we're judging these kids all the time without spending much time in their shoes.

I think you have to be aware all the time that, as

much as you wish it weren't true, university campuses aren't any different from anywhere else in America. There are going to be differences in the ways white people and black people see things. If you're white and you're coaching at the top levels of college football or college basketball, you're going to find yourself standing in the middle of a locker room in which you're in the minority. How can you not be sensitive to what black players are thinking?

During the '95 season, one of my black players came to me and asked to be excused from a Monday practice so he could take part in the Million Man March in Washington, D.C. I had been watching the news leading up to the march. So I had heard about Louis Farrakhan, who was organizing it. I knew some people didn't think much of him and some people did. But I kind of liked what I heard about the purposes of the march, about men taking responsibility for themselves, their families, their communities. That's certainly what I preach, and it's certainly what I'd like players to take away from their experiences here.

I talked to this player in my office for a while, because I wanted to make sure he was sincere about the purposes of the march. I asked him a lot of questions, and he kept telling me how important he thought it was to be there.

Finally, I told him, "You can go. But you're the only one who can go. You can represent other Florida State players up there."

I didn't want to get into a whole thing about, "Well, if he can go, why can't I?" If I didn't watch it, the practice would be disrupted and the team would be divided.

Well, it turns out this player gets hurt and can't go to Washington. And Monday, the day of the Million Man March, rolls around, and I start hearing from my assistants that a lot of the black players are talking about not going to practice so they can watch the march on TV. Now, I'm really concerned. I can't have some players showing up and some not. So I call a meeting in my office.

I think about twenty black players are in there, and one by one, they tell me how important they think it is that they honor the Million Man March by taking the day off from practice. I turn to each one: "Do you really believe this or are you just saying this because the other guy said it?" And every one of them tells me they think it's important.

So I called off the practice. I heard coaches at some other schools disciplined players for not going to practice that day. But I'm convinced I did the right thing. You have to listen to your players. And you have to preserve the team. I couldn't ignore something that important to these players. It would have just festered and caused problems somewhere down the line.

TERRY: You know we get criticism from another direction on these issues. Some people see all these great black athletes going to overwhelmingly white universities and say they're just being used.

BOBBY: My best argument is that, of all the places in America where black people are going to get a fair shot at success, sports must be near the top of the list. That's why there are so many great black athletes, because black kids have gravitated toward something in which prejudice is likely to be overwhelmed by something more powerful—the need to win.

That doesn't say great things about the rest of society, I know. And it doesn't mean coaches are free of the prejudices that infect everybody else. What opens up so many opportunities in sports is that it's in coaches' selfish interest to find the best athletes available, no matter what color they are.

I remember recruiting black players when I was a coach at West Virginia. There were always some old alums who wanted to know how many I was going to let on the team. They had a quota in their heads. Well, I tell you, you keep winning games and those old guys get color-blind pretty quick, and those quotas get stuck in their pockets.

In recent years, I've heard criticism from our fans, too, that our players were doing too much finger-pointing and celebrating. And it just so happened that all of the kids fans complained about were black.

It's a very touchy thing trying to explain to players that age that they have to change what they consider part of their game, part of the style they grew up imitating—without it appearing that it's the white colleges, coaches, and administrators coming down on black players. And I understand where they're coming from.

TERRY: The first thing I try to tell our kids is whatever things they did in high school aren't necessarily bad. But now they're in a different place. We represent Auburn and Auburn people. A lot of our people have been around this school, this football program, for seventy-five years. And I want us to try to react in a way that makes our fans proud.

I tell players it's the same problem they'll have to face when they graduate and have to go work for somebody in a bank. They say you have to wear a dark suit, a white shirt, and wing-tip shoes every day. If you don't, you can't work there—no matter where you came from, what you like to do. You'll either not go into that line of business or you'll wear a dark suit and a white shirt.

If we really are trying to learn lessons that sports teach, this is one of them: "We're going to put our individual desires aside for the good of the team, for the good of the university and our fans."

There's no getting around the fact that Auburn is located in a very conservative area. I've got to make a decision who I'm going to recruit and how they're going to fit into that environment. I'll go into parts of the country that are not nearly as conservative, where players are accustomed to the antics that are considered showboating and taunting in our part of the country. And I've got to convince those kids that while there may not be anything wrong with all that, they have to find other ways to express excitement and emotion if they're going to play at Auburn. Luckily, a lot of parents like the idea that I'm encouraging their sons to learn that they can't always be their own masters, that sometimes they have to toe the company line.

BOBBY: Yes, but the company owes them something back, as well.

A lot of athletic departments have tremendous invest-
ments in academic support and counseling programs.
They were forced into that because so many of the athletes who come from tough backgrounds just weren't
making it in college. When people pointed fingers at
schools for allowing players to fall by the wayside, the
NCAA started requiring regular graduation rate reports
from schools. And suddenly, millions of dollars got
spent for tutors, learning labs, and academic counselors.

These programs benefit athletes from all sports. At
Florida State, for instance, we have seventy-five tutors
and four full-time counselors available to something like
four hundred athletes. But as far as I know, all the
money to run these academic support centers at schools
like ours comes out of athletic department budgets and
from booster funds generated by the football and basketball programs.

It's turned out to be a pretty good investment. These
days, many of the most successful schools in athletics
are also among the best at helping athletes get degrees.

Take Florida State, for instance. Out of the '88 class
of football recruits—as we write this, that's the most
recent class monitored by the NCAA—we graduated 71
percent of our players within six years. That's eight per-
centage points higher than the six-year grad rate for
FSU's '88 freshman class as a whole.

And how about the black players, whom we're
accused of exploiting because so many are so unpre-
pared for college academics? Well, it turns out we're
doing a much better job keeping black football players
working toward degrees than the rest of the university is

doing with black male students overall. In that '88 class, we graduated 79 percent of our black scholarship players in six years. Of all black male students entering Florida State as freshmen in '88, only 49 percent graduated over the same period.

Of course, grad rates go up and down from year to year, because a program like ours is very vulnerable to losing kids early to the NFL. A player who leaves in his junior year and gets a million bucks to play pro football considers himself a success. A lot of other people do, too. But if he hasn't graduated, he counts against us in the reports we send to the NCAA. In the '89 class, for instance, we gave scholarships to twenty-two guys. Nine of them went on to the NFL. Some left early. So when we start adding up grad rates from that year, we may not look so good. That's why we stay after former players to come back and finish, even if they're having great careers in the pros. Right now, we have about ten former FSU players on NFL rosters who come back in the off-season to take courses toward their degrees.

And though you hear plenty of stories about guys who play out their eligibility, then drop out, you don't hear nearly enough about players like Felix Harris.

Felix was a highly recruited fullback in that '88 class. A lot of schools wanted him, because he was such a star in high school in central Florida. A lot would have taken him, too, even though his grades and test scores were low. By today's rules, we couldn't even accept a guy with Felix's high school record. But back then we could extend the scholarship if we let him sit out a year to get his bearings in school.

Well, ol' Felix was never a star student, but he was as determined as anybody I've ever seen. Though it was a struggle all the way, he kept himself out of academic trouble and was able to come out to play in his sophomore year. The only thing was, he had the misfortune to be the fullback behind Edgar Bennett and William Floyd, both of whom were going to be NFL stars. I think Felix got maybe fifteen carries his whole career.

A lot of kids have a tough time accepting that kind of backup role. They go back home at Christmas and over the summers, and everybody rides them: "What do you mean, you ain't starting? What are you doing up there working that hard if you ain't got a chance to impress NFL scouts and get drafted in the pros?" You just know he was hearing that.

But Felix hung in there, both on the practice field and in the classroom. He logged a lot of time with tutors and counselors. And by the time he finished up his eligibility, he not only had graduated, he was on his way to a master's degree in social work. Now, he's got a solid career counseling kids.

Much of what Felix accomplished had to do with the kind of person he is. But I don't have a doubt in the world that football in general, and a scholarship to Florida State University in particular, made Felix's success a whole lot more likely.

When critics start talking about how we exploit athletes, I wish more people would think of players like Felix Harris. And when fans complain that athletes these days are different than the old days, that they're wasting their opportunities and showing disrespect for their schools, I wish somebody would point out that a lot of our kids—despite coming from circumstances a whole lot more challenging—accomplish more in the time they have than many of the students around them.

12

Managing Fear

BOBBY: There's this debate among coaches about what motivates you more, the determination to win or the fear of losing. One guy will say, "I win because I just love that feeling. I've just got to win to get that feeling."

Now, I'm the opposite. I say, "I've got to win because I'm so afraid of losing. I hate that feeling of losing so much I'll do just about anything to escape it."

TERRY: I've heard you talk about that a lot, Dad, and I think I know exactly what you mean. But I'm not sure people listening to you always understand. I think it boils down to how you use that fear, what it motivates you to do.

There are people out there who are so afraid of failing they never jump into the game. Fear paralyzes them.

It puts them on the sidelines. They are too frightened of losing to even try. They aren't going to go into that boss's office and ask for that raise. They aren't going to risk investing in their own ideas. And if they're coaches, they aren't going to jump out there and call a critical play on fourth and inches, because they're afraid it won't work and will make them look stupid.

That ain't you, Dad.

We're so used to hearing motivational speakers and psychologists warn us about the fear of failure we're probably reluctant to acknowledge what a motivator fear is. We all like that whistling-by-the-graveyard stuff, where even if you don't feel all that confident, you fake it. Yet some of the most successful people in business and sports are pretty good at using fear to push themselves into working harder, preparing better, and, once they're in the heat of battle, to jump on every opportunity.

BOBBY: I guess it's a matter of how you express it. The guy who says he's motivated because he loves to win may mean he's so afraid to lose it amounts to the same thing. I do know that I'm more afraid of losing than anything. But I also know by now that the fear is a pretty useful thing. Because of it, I never take anything for granted.

At the beginning of every game week during the season, all I've got are worries and questions. I get my first look at the opposing team on film, and I'm asking: "How are we ever gonna block that linebacker? What if they slip into this or that coverage? Man, don't they look better than last year?"

What that does is force us all into considering every detail of a game plan, whether we're about to face Florida or some team that hasn't won a game.

On the night before every game, I sit down with my offensive coordinator and maybe a couple of other coaches. I want them to convince me we have a plan for every "what if" situation: First play to start the game. Third and long, deep in our own territory. Fourth and goal to win the game.

I'm used to working that way now. And because most of them have been with me a long time, my assistants are comfortable with the way we structure our preparations. Fear, fear of losing, drives the whole thing. And as funny as it sounds, it's turned out to be a pretty successful approach.

TERRY: What we're doing is allowing a certain amount of stress to stimulate us. It's the old bell curve of anxiety. If you have some anxiety, your performance goes up; if you have too much, your performance drops off.

It seems to work especially well in football. I was never a great baseball player, partly because I wanted to win so badly that when I got to the plate I would tighten up too much. I would choke that danged bat until my knuckles turned white. That level of anxiety is not what you need to be a good batter against a good pitcher. You have to be more relaxed to react properly.

My personality was always better suited for football, where a certain amount of tension and anxiety can heighten your performance.

BOBBY: Yeah, but too much tension can mess you up in football, too—especially on offense. That's why, if we win the coin toss to start the game, I always choose to kick the ball to the other guys. I would rather have their offense on the field first. Let their quarterback and running backs and receivers deal with the jitters.

When everything in your body is telling you to run as fast as you can and hit somebody, I think you're better off trying to take the ball away from the other guys than trying to hold on to it and move it down the field. So I would much rather have our defensive team out on the field first. I figure that's one way to get a double advantage from the anxiety: It's something they have to overcome and something we can use.

TERRY: The danger for coaches probably comes in a game where it's going down to the wire. I know you and I have talked a lot in the past about handling the pressures of big games, where it seems like you can win it or lose it on every play and where you feel you just can't afford to make a mistake. The tighter the score and the closer to the final gun you get, the higher the pressure. And if you're not careful, your fear of losing can make you lose your flare for play-calling. You lose your imagination. You stop doing the things that got you there.

BOBBY: I don't think there's a coach in the world who hasn't gone through that. Certainly, I have—even though we have a reputation as having one of the most wide-open offensive games in college football. After a couple of those gut-wrenching losses to Miami, for instance, I asked my assistants to go back and look at our play-calling: "Was I too conservative? Did we lose our nerve when we got down to the end?"

You had better ask yourselves those questions—and answer them honestly—or you'll stop improving. And there's only one direction to go when you stop getting better.

TERRY: In '95, I got a dose of that, when I saw we were going to have to change our offense or risk losing big. That fear sent me back to the film of '93, when everything was working right. It sent me to your film, Dad, when I was trying to figure out how to mix what we were doing with what you were doing.

I had a tape machine put into my home so that when I couldn't sleep at night, I could get up and watch game tapes. The only thing I know to do in those situations, when I fear what might come next if I don't come up with a plan, is to work harder.

If eight hours worked the week before, then why not sixteen this week? Pretty soon, I'm working around the clock, not getting any sleep and—if I don't watch it—exhausting my staff and messing up other parts of my life.

It's another example of how my drive works for and against me. If I have another season like '95 and handle it in the same way, I can forget about my longtime goals of coaching for twenty or thirty more years. I'll be dead before I'm fifty.

BOBBY: When I was your age, Terry, I was the same way. It would kill me so much when we lost I would double up on my preparations for the next game. Then,

I would double up again. But you can't go on like that for long.

I know this is easy for me to say. But you have got to keep this thing in perspective. Losing ain't the end of the world.

And when you're a head coach, you've especially got to get that message out to your staff and your players. If they see you wallowing in self-pity after a loss or sense you're afraid, you can forget about getting them prepared for the next game.

Part of being a head coach is playing the actor. You've got to pretend you have all the confidence in the world even when you're shaking in your boots and even when you're torn up inside over a big loss.

You remember our '91 loss to Miami in Tallahassee. That was the famous "wide right" game, when our last-minute field goal attempt sailed just a sliver to the right and we lost it all.

We went into that game 10–0 and No. 1 in the polls. We were hurting physically, but a win against Miami would have given us the momentum to go into Gainesville against Florida two weeks later favored to beat them and to play in a bowl for the national championship.

The slogan our kids chose for that season was "No excuses," and they had it plastered everywhere. If we lose, there can be no excuses. "We have the talent and experience. We are *supposed* to win."

Man, that's always a dangerous attitude. It makes a loss seem an even bigger failure. It makes it seem like everything you believed is now wrong. And the fear comes rushing in: "Is this whole thing over? Can we ever win again?"

That loss tore me up, but when I saw what it did to the fans and to the players and even to some on my staff, I got worried that we couldn't pull out of it in time to get the work done for Florida. I called meetings with the players. We did everything we could at practices to show enthusiasm. We lectured and yelled and joked with 'em, trying to get everybody believing again.

I think sportswriters and fans like to imagine that you can stand up in front of a team at times like that and give some speech that turns everything around. That's what happens in the movies. But the truth is, about the only thing you can do is remind your players of things they should already know. You remind them how talented they are, how far they've come, and how hard they've worked. You remind them of all the times they've won, sometimes when they had to come from behind. You remind them of how much they owe their teammates.

The big thing you have working for you—and this is something about sports that just can't be underestimated—is that you get to play again. There's the next game or the next season. And the one thing you don't have to remind your team is how terrible it feels to lose. Nobody wants to feel that way again.

Well, in '91, after that loss to Miami, we had a week off before we had to go to Gainesville. It took every bit of that for the players to get out of their funk. But we were so banged up from a long season that we probably weren't physically ready to go up against a fired-up team like Florida. We lost. Yet despite all our troubles, when it came down to the end of that game, we were driving for what would have been the winning score. I think that was enough to help us begin an end-of-season comeback, because we were able to put together enough of an effort in the Cotton Bowl to hold off Texas A&M and go 11–2 for the year.

There were a lot of young players on that '91 team. And I think they learned something that helped us win the national championship two years later.

Ten games into that '93 season we lost another big game, this one to Notre Dame at their place. All of us— me, the staff, the kids—were determined not to let that one derail us. No one had to be reminded what it felt like in that locker room after the Florida game in '91. We were still ranked high enough that we had a shot at the title. But we still had two games to go, including our usual end-of-the-year game against Florida.

Well, we had North Carolina State in the next game and beat them 62–3. Then, we went back to Florida's home field for the first time since that '91 loss. We beat the Gators 33–21 and had enough votes in the poll to get into a No. 1 vs. No. 2 showdown against Nebraska in the Orange Bowl, where we won by a whisker.

Fear is a motivator. It's sure motivated me through the years. I think fear of losing motivated some of our players to that national title.

TERRY: The great thing about this job, something that separates us from a lot of business managers, is that you get to do something about your anxiety. You get to plan an attack. And then you get to go out and practice what you've planned to build your confidence back up.

BOBBY: Yes, and the best way to prepare for pressure is to practice pressure situations over and over. We practice from the negative side a lot, taking turns putting our offense, then our defense in the hole with time running out. One play to win the game. What's it going to be?

What we want to build is poise under pressure, poise under pressure. I just don't think there can be anything more important than that.

The one-minute drill, where you practice coming from behind at the end of a game, is something that's a regular part of practices for most teams. I guess you could call that a stress-induced offense.

It fits so well with our style that we've turned the one-minute drill, with the quarterback taking the ball out of the shotgun formation, into a sixty-minute offense. No huddle. Just snap the ball and move it down the field. Hurry up, hurry up, hurry up. It drives people nuts.

Usually, if you find yourself in that kind of offensive situation in a game, it means you're losing and time's running out. But we've become famous using it from the opening kickoff. Charlie Ward won the Heisman Trophy quarterbacking that offense. We won the national championship.

Now, think about that. I don't think you're going to find a better example of creating a winning system out of a strategy that was originally intended for folks who are scared to death they're about to lose a football game.

13

LEARNING TO WIN

BOBBY: Like most coaches—and business leaders, too, I suppose—I believe that winning is something you have to learn how to do. I'm talking about consistent winning, now. Not the one-shot victory that you enjoy for a moment before you go back to losing or breaking even.

When you're a kid playing sports and you've got talent for the game, winning doesn't seem all that mysterious. If you've got the right guys on your team and you play hard, you're gonna win more than you lose. Now I still believe, more than anything else, in working hard. I made up my mind early in my career that was the one thing I had absolute control over. I figured I might get outmanned and outsmarted a time or two, but I was determined to make sure I never got outprepared. I still preach that: Don't let anybody outwork you. But the thing is, working hard, by itself, is not enough.

There are a lot of people out there, a lot of coaches and teams, working as hard as humanly possible. And they ain't winning consistently.

So how do you learn to win? The first thing you need to do is surround yourself with talent. Put yourself in a position to win. As much as I love gritty overachievers, a team full of great athletes ably prepared will have the advantage every time.

From the beginning, I gravitated toward talented people. I wanted to copy their habits and their ideas. I didn't get to play football at a major college for a Bear Bryant or a Joe Paterno, but I was lucky to take over the coaching job at my alma mater, Howard, in 1959, one year after Coach Bryant took over at Alabama down the road in Tuscaloosa. He was my hero anyway, because of what he'd done at Kentucky and Texas A&M. Then, he comes back to my home state, and I'm able to watch what he does. I learned so much in those days watching him go from nothing to national champion.

Every time I got a chance, I would head over to Tuscaloosa to spend time with Coach Bryant and his assistants. Gene Stallings, who went on to become the Alabama head coach and win a national championship, was a twenty-five-year-old assistant back in those days. I was twenty-nine and a new head coach. He was young and eager to talk. I was young and eager to soak up everything. And we would talk football all day.

TERRY: For Tommy, Jeff, and I, learning from winners has always meant drawing on our experiences watching you. You have won so consistently, I think that created an expectation in us that we could do the same if we approached things the way you did.

Although I don't think this is much of a problem for those of us who really know you, some people may have noticed a contradiction in what you say and what you do. You like to talk about how conservative you are, how scared to death you are of losing, but I don't think you could have done what you've done without taking big risks.

You and Mom had already had four of us kids when you were working for almost nothing at small colleges. You left your home state and a secure job at your alma mater to become an assistant in Tallahassee. You left that for what could have been a lateral move in West Virginia.

When you took over as head coach at Florida State, the school was close to dropping the whole program. There was no conference, no tradition, no regional image—let alone a national identity. To lots of folks in Florida, FSU was still "the girls school."

So you become the "Road Warrior." You built a national reputation by taking your team into the home stadiums of big-name schools that wouldn't even return the favor of coming to Tallahassee. More risky stuff.

You beat a lot of those big-name teams on TV. And even though we all know you as a fanatic for basic football, for practice-till-you're-perfect blocking and tackling, you attracted all this attention with trick plays—double reverses and hidden-ball gimmicks. People started calling you the "River Boat Gambler." You were the guy liable to do anything, anytime, anywhere on the field.

How do you reconcile all that with the image you have of yourself as this 'fraid-to-lose conservative?

BOBBY: I'm not backing off 'fraid-to-lose one bit. The fact is, I am so terrified of losing, I want to hit the other guys before they get at me. I want to keep them off balance. I want to score first and keep scoring until there's not a chance in the world they can catch us.

Now, here's the part that must seem so contradictory. I feel like I've got to risk losing to keep on winning. There's just no way around it. To win consistently, you've got to put yourself in a position where you're liable to lose.

When I first came to Florida State and we put all those big-name teams on our schedule, that forced us to recruit better and practice harder. We had to play a little over our heads just to stay on the same field with some of those teams. Of course, because we had the advantage of being underdogs so often, every game we won helped our reputation and improved our players' confidence. Looking good on national television, throwing the ball all over the field and pulling those double reverses, didn't hurt us a bit when we were recruiting those high school stars, either.

So the calculated risk paid off. Jumping into a schedule that demanded so much of us gave us the chance to get better every game, every season. And there is no way you can understate how crucial that is. There are only two ways to go in this business: You get better or you get passed up. And that applies whether you're coming off an 0–11 season or the national championship.

I catch the dickens from my alums and boosters for

keeping Miami on our schedule. If we hadn't played them, we might have gone undefeated and won a national championship two or three more times in the '80s and early '90s. Notre Dame took Miami off its regular schedule. Penn State stopped playing them. Even Florida dropped them. So why do I think it's so important to tee up with that bunch every year?

Well, it goes back to that same philosophy: You cannot expect to win consistently without improving every season. And you can't improve unless you test yourself against the best. For most of the years that our alums were pleading with us to drop Miami, the national championship could have been decided by the games we played against one another. A whole string of them turned out to be "Games of the Century." Isn't that what we want—the chance to play for the national championship each year?

You are shaped by your competition. You measure yourself against your toughest rival. Just having those guys on our schedule meant we had to ask ourselves: "Are we preparing smart enough to beat Miami? Are we practicing hard enough?"

TERRY: The Alabama game amounts to about the same for us. It is just about impossible—certainly for our fans—not to define Auburn's success by how we do against Alabama. And that brings up an interesting question about choosing styles of winning.

Like a lot of great football teams, Alabama is going to live and die with its defense. In seven or eight games a year, they're physically going to whip people and be happy to win 14–7 or 10–3. They're going to do that so much that they're going to put themselves into position to win the conference title season after season and compete for the national championship every other year.

Often as not, the kind of game a team like Alabama—or Penn State or Nebraska or Miami—forces is one of those tight, nervous affairs where one misstep wins or loses it. You've got to play four great quarters, controlling the ball and not turning it over.

So if you know that's the kind of game you've got to play to win the two or three toughest games on your schedule, then why in the world would you go out there and throw it every down for the other eight games? Especially when you know you're probably going to win whether you run it every time or pass it every time.

When you get to the big game where you've got to play ball control and no turnovers, you suddenly are in a game that's not your style. Maybe in all those games where you're clearly better than your opponents you'd be better off averaging 28 points instead of 50 and running the heck out of that ball. Then, when you face a team that won't let you throw it all over the place, you're ready.

The question is, what's the best championship offense to have? Is it the one that scores the most or the one that prepares you for the games when you're playing to win it all?

If you're an underdog five or six times a year and you just don't ever have the talent the big boys have, this isn't an issue. But it's a question worth addressing at these top programs, where, if you do everything right, you have a chance every year to get down to a season that's a matter of two games.

BOBBY: Well, son, I have never allowed myself the luxury of believing I didn't need to score all the points I possibly could. I might have grown up in the era where you tried to grind it out on offense, then rely on your defense to keep the other guys out of the end zone; but it didn't take me long to come around to the idea that you must attack every chance you get.

First of all, it just suited my disposition. And I suspect it's the same for you.

Now, I know with the kind of year your young defense had in '95, you've been worrying about keeping the other team out of the end zone. But fretting over the defense is not my strong suit, and it ain't yours either. We're both little guys who learned pretty fast in life that you've got to hit the big ones first—then hightail it out of there.

In Mickey Andrews, I've got the best defensive coordinator around. And he's there so I don't have to worry about that side of the ball. He does stuff I don't even pretend to understand. He scares me to death substituting linemen and linebackers and defensive backs the whole game. Sometimes I can't bear to look. But he knows what he's doing, and he knows what I want: Get me that ball!

JEFF: No coach is going to argue against having a great defense. Great defenses win championships. But you've got to do things right on offense or you can't take advantage of what a good defense can do for you.

Me, I would be trying to score as many points as I could every game. And that means passing the ball.

With our talent at Florida State, we can get into the I

formation and run sprint draws and toss sweeps all day. It would put people to sleep, but we could win most of our games—provided we played great defense. Or we can score 60 or 70 points a game, have a lot of fun, and still play great defense.

I vote for the excitement. That's what people want to see.

BOBBY: If I ever needed evidence that what I needed to be paying attention to was offense I got it in 1970, my very first year as a head coach at West Virginia.

It started out easy. I win my first game against Lou Holtz, who was then at William and Mary. We beat them 43–7, and I think we were still trying to score there at the end, and Lou was furious.

Now, the story he tells—though I don't remember exactly what we said to each other—is that when he started complaining about us running up the score, I said something like, "Lou, the way I see it, my job is to score. It's your job to hold my score down."

If I didn't say it, I wish I had. Because I believe it. And I believe it more today than I did then because of what happened later that season.

Anyway, after that win against William and Mary, we're rolling. We win maybe three in a row. "This is something," I'm thinking. "I'm a genius. We can't lose."

Now we get to the point in the schedule where we're playing Duke and Pitt back to back. Duke, back in those days, was better than West Virginia. They had given us some pretty good lickings. But in 1970, we're undefeated going into that game, and it was going to be at home; so we were favored by three points or so.

Well, we play that game and it's a battle. We are down 13–7 in the fourth quarter, and it just doesn't feel like our defense can hold 'em. With about seven minutes to go, we get the ball and we drive down to their 31-yard line. But we're having a terrible time making yards.

We come up with a fourth down and 4 yards to go on their 31. So I call my defensive coordinator over.

I grab him by the collar and pull him close so he can hear me. The crowd is screaming and I'm shouting to him: "If we go for this and don't make it, can you stop 'em right there? Can you stop 'em so we can get the ball back?"

Real quiet-like, he says, "I don't know."

Now, this is the opposite thing you want to hear at a moment like that. You're expecting, "You're darn right we'll stop 'em, coach. Go for it!"

But what I get from him is, "I don't know."

Well, I decide to punt on the 31-yard line. Now, everybody in the stands is ticked. They're booing my punter as he trots out there. But I'm thinking, "This is the way those great old coaches of the past would do it. We'll pin 'em back inside their own five, get the ball back, and have plenty of time to score."

So the punter goes out and boots the dadgum ball clear out of the end zone. I mean, he kicks it a mile! Imagine my sick feeling as I'm watching that ball sail. And now the boos really crank up.

Duke takes over the ball at the 20 and is able to make a couple of first downs, and we never get close again. Time runs out and we lose by six points.

I learned a lesson there. You just can't take anything for granted.

Nobody thought to remind that punter to kick it out of bounds inside the five. You just assume he understands that's what he has to do in that situation. But you can't assume a kid knows what's in a coach's mind. You've got to tell him what you want.

And you can't assume you'll always get another chance to score. You've got to seize the opportunities when you've got them.

Now, if I had that same choice, I wouldn't punt it. I'd go for it on fourth down. You get that close near the end of the game, you had better take advantage of it.

Punting would have been the thing to do if you coached in 1940, but not in 1970, and certainly not in 1995.

TERRY: It's funny how closely that situation paralleled one we had in the '95 Georgia game. We were leading midway through the fourth quarter by 6 points. But neither defense was having much luck stopping the other offense. We were driving and got to about their 35-yard line when we stalled, and it was fourth down.

I turn to my defensive coordinator, and he says, "Go for it, Terry. We can stop 'em."

What we both knew, though, was that I had better go for it. The way Georgia had been moving up and down the field, if we gave them back the ball, there was a pretty good chance they could go 65 yards in the six minutes left. What my defensive coordinator really meant but left unsaid was, "In this situation, our best defense is going to be our offense. We've got to go for it!"

Telling me to go for it was exactly the right thing to say. He was expressing faith in our offense without betraying his own guys. It was what I needed to hear. Because if he had told me he was worried about keeping Georgia out of the end zone from 65 yards out, I might have punted to make them go 95 yards.

We went for it and made the first down and ate up enough clock to win the game. In that case, offense was our defense. It kept us in control of the game.

BOBBY: Boy, is that a crucial lesson. If I didn't get the point when we lost to Duke, I sure got it in the next game we played that year. That was that famous Pitt game where we lost 36–35 after being up 35–8 at the half. That's the last time I sat on the ball. You go through something like that one time, you don't ever mind people getting on you for running the score up. You start to think, "I can't ever have enough points!"

The thing is, you have to learn to win when you're ahead.

Doesn't that sound strange? If you're ahead, you're gonna win if you just hold on, aren't you? Well, not if you stop playing to win. You have to play till the end as hard as you played in the beginning.

For most of my playing and coaching career I had that wonderful advantage of being an underdog. I was the little kid in the neighborhood daring the big boys. I was the coach of independents in a region dominated by powerful conferences. I took over a team at the "girls school."

But you can't make a career out of being an underdog. It's a transition phase. If you win enough, you lose your chance to be David, and you start having to be Goliath. You become the one who makes everybody else the underdog.

Notre Dame got to that point years ago. So did Alabama, Oklahoma, Miami, and now us at Florida State. Yet every one of us have been upset in key games when we were supposed to be on championship runs. It is just so hard to win every time you're supposed to— much harder, I think, than to win a game or two you're not supposed to.

TERRY: That's something we're experiencing, too. In that 11–0 year in '93 and the 9-1-1 season that followed we were on NCAA probation. No TV. No bowl game. We were everybody's favorite underdog.

Every game seemed like a miracle. I think we came from behind to win something like eight times that first year.

Then we come back in '95 picked to be in the Top 10 nationally. And suddenly, we're the team to beat. Louisiana State puts a record crowd in that stadium to see us on a Saturday night. The whole state of Arkansas is going crazy when we come up there. And we lose both games.

BOBBY: Get used to it, son. That's one of those problems you're going to have to solve over and over. You can count up on one hand the number of coaches who have put together long undefeated strings.

I got a humiliating introduction to the top-dog blues back in 1988. That was the first year we'd been picked No. 1 to start the season, and we were flying high for our opening game down in the Orange Bowl against Miami.

In the off-season some of our players thought it would be a great idea to make a rap record and video. They convinced me to go along with it, even though all my instincts argued against doing anything to thump your chest before you've done anything. They were already heavy into the thing when I got wind of it, and I thought it might hurt morale if I made them quit.

So out comes this rap song just before the season begins. And it's playing everywhere on the radio: "We're gonna get you, Miami . . . And then we're comin' after you, Gators . . . and on and on." Man, when I heard that on the radio, it sounded lots worse than I imagined.

Well, ol' Jimmy Johnson, who was coaching the Hurricanes then, gets hold of the record and plays it about a million times for his players while they're practicing. The whole off-season he had been moaning about all the players he lost and how it was going to be a rebuilding year in Miami. All the usual poor-mouthing stuff that I should have been immune to after all my years in Southern football.

So we go down there and prance into the Orange Bowl with Burt Reynolds and everybody else on hand to watch us smear the Hurricanes. And we ran into the worst ambush you can imagine. We got beat 31–0. Totally humiliated.

You should have seen what all the Monday-morning quarterbacks had to say about that one. We're No. 1 and can't even make it past the first week.

After that game, we won eleven games straight. I'm proud that we redeemed ourselves that way. But don't

think anybody who was at that game in Miami ever for-
got about how tough it is when the underdog advantage
swings to the other side.

And if you notice, there ain't been many rap songs
out of Florida State since then, either.

14

Coping with Losing

TERRY: In a lot of ways, starting off my Division I-A career with an undefeated season was one of the worst things that could have happened to me. After that, things could only get worse.

My second season, we lose only one game. And I'm still riding high.

Then we get to that deafening stadium in Baton Rouge three games into the '95 season, and reality sets in. We're not going to pull out every close game in the last seconds. We're not going to beat everybody every week.

The positive side of my nature tells me losses present opportunities to solve problems to make you better. My insecurity nags at me that if I don't fix this pretty quick I'll be looking for another job.

Dad, I know losing hits you about as hard as anybody

in this business. But you seem to have a system to cope with it.

BOBBY: I have a regular routine I go through when I lose. I can't change it. I probably shouldn't try at this stage, since it works as a kind of therapy for me. But I've often wondered what might happen if I could just escape after a loss, walk off the field and into some other country where nobody knows or cares anything about football, where it's a different time and people speak a different language and nobody recognizes me.

If that's not a coach's fantasy, I don't know what is.

What I have instead is this ritual that I've gone through for years and years. It helps me get through the pain and on to what I have to do to get ready to play again.

The first thing I have to do after a loss is talk to the team. I say the obvious things about good effort and "we'll get 'em next week." I don't dwell on our mistakes. I try to point out the positives. But they're not listening, and neither am I. We're all numb.

Then I have to talk to the media. And while some coaches hate that part worse than anything, it helps me to go back through the painful parts of the game and to do my best to explain—even though at that point I don't have a real grasp of what happened, just the memory of a few plays where it felt like everything went wrong.

Confronting those questions helps me. There's a kind of release there that you can't get if you just keep it bottled up. I talk and talk. I may joke a little. But it's strictly gallows humor. That noose is so tight around my neck I can feel it choking me.

Everyone says, "Boy, ol' Bowden really knows how to handle this stuff. He walks off the field after getting beat on national television and cracks a joke. He really has things in perspective."

But down deep, it's killing me. It's just killing me.

I go back to my office and greet whoever's waiting for me there. But I'm on automatic pilot now. A writer comes by, or I do a TV or radio interview. And I get to walk through it all one more time.

I go home. There's a game on TV, but it's a blur. I sit there and watch it, but I'm not really paying attention. If there are people in the house, I'll smile, say something to them. But I'm really hoping they'll go away. I don't want to talk to anybody.

After everyone's gone, I usually sit up until I can't stand it any longer. I'll watch a late-night taped replay of the game if there's one on. And finally, when I just can't keep my eyes open any longer, I'll stumble off to bed. At that point, my body's exhausted, because I probably haven't slept in two nights. I never have been able to sleep much the night before a game.

So then I fall asleep. But I'll wake up two, three, four times during the night, and it's the most awful feeling. I wake up, draw this deep breath, like a gasp. And there's this painful voice in me: YOU LOST! . . . YOU LOST! . . . YOU LOST!

I try to go back to sleep again, but maybe fifteen minutes later, I wake up again: YOU LOST! . . . YOU LOST! . . . YOU LOST!

Now, I know this is silly. It's an overreaction. It shouldn't be this way. But it is.

Finally, after an exasperating night of not really sleeping, not really wanting to wake up, it's five A.M. and time to get up and go tape my TV show. I get to watch the game on film, previewing it for the show. And now, for the first time, I can look at what happened as a coach and not as a victim of some calamity that befell us the day before.

I begin to see positive things. I think, "Hey, we don't look as bad as I thought! . . . If that guy had made his block . . . If this guy had wrapped his arms on the tackle . . . We could have stopped them there . . . We could have scored here."

Now, I'm getting back to reality. "We could have won that dadgum game," I'm thinking. "I know how to fix those mistakes. We'll put this play in. We'll make this or that adjustment, and we'll shock 'em next week."

I go home, feeling a little better. And then I meet with the press again for my Sunday news conference, where I get to sit down, mostly with the regulars who cover us week to week, and go through it all again.

Now, I really am more relaxed. The jokes aren't so forced. "Yeah," I can say, "we stunk it up in a couple of places. Here's what we were doing wrong. And here's how we'll fix it."

Then I go by the office and pick up films of the next opponent. Sunday night, I can sleep for the first time. The loss is behind me. Everything now is pointed to that next opponent.

TERRY: The next opponent. Have you ever thought what it would be like not to have somebody to play next?

BOBBY: Whew, that would be terrible. I think that's one reason why I put so much effort into winning those bowl games. Bowls are supposed to be fun for everybody, rewards for successful seasons. And I try to make it so our kids can enjoy them. But I'm determined to win those games. We haven't lost a bowl game since 1980.

You lose that last game and you have to live the entire off-season with that taste in your mouth. You win it, and you have momentum going into the next year.

TERRY: I bet lots of people will be surprised to hear how losing still affects you after all these years of winning.

BOBBY: When I say I'm afraid of losing, I mean it. If we win, that's great. But it doesn't take you as high as losing takes you low. After wins, it's "Enjoy yourself tonight, 'cause tomorrow it's all over." You have to point yourself toward that next game. And as soon as a day passes, here come those pangs again: "Can you win again?"

You do get better at handling the losses, though. I think it's like getting hit with a hammer. The pain hurts so much the first time. The second may hurt even more because it falls on that soft spot. Then comes the third and the fourth and so on. And the pain gets duller and duller and duller.

I can handle it better at my age, but it took some getting used to. When I was coaching at South Georgia College and lost my very first game as a head coach, it nearly killed me.

I think we won the first two that year, then we lost the third game. We got killed 60-something to maybe 20. I didn't want to see anybody. I crept back to South Georgia, and the next day I didn't even want to go out the door for fear of somebody seeing me and pointing a finger: "YOU LOST!"

Now, who in the heck cared whether South Georgia College won a game or not? The local paper didn't even write it up. And most of the people at the school didn't care either. We'd have maybe a thousand people show up at games.

But oh, it killed me. I even considered getting out of coaching. "How can I possibly go on if it's going to feel this way when I lose?" Like all young coaches, I thought, "I'm the answer to coaching, baby." I must have thought I was going to go undefeated all my life.

When I was forty, I wanted to be a great coach, one of the biggest of all time. And I was always thinking, "I can't make it if I lose this game." But now, I've won so many games that kind of pressure is off.

But isn't it interesting that I'm still driven by that fear? I still wake up with that awful voice in my ear the night after a loss. The difference now is there's another voice saying, "You're secure. Your job and your family are not in jeopardy. The world ain't going to cave in."

TERRY: Most of the times when you lose it's because the other team is a little better than you. That's not something fans like to hear, but it's the truth.

The key, I think, is to make sure you take something away from those losses that can give you a better chance to win. Try to salvage anything. As a coach, I've learned a lot about that by watching you, Dad. Your postgame rituals may be something to help you release the pain of losing, but I think they also plant the seeds for preparing to win again. If you win, what you say to the press can just add to the victory. If you lose, you can gain back some of what you lost on the field.

I remember in '94 when we had the big win in Gainesville against Florida. We had gone undefeated in '93 and were still winning them all in '94, when Steve Spurrier, the Florida coach, was getting bugged to death by reporters: "What about Auburn, what about Auburn?" And he finally popped off something about the easy schedule we had.

Well, that sound bite was on every highlight show and game preview before we go into Gainesville. So after we beat the Gators and the crowd is going crazy, I'm walking off the field and the ABC reporter grabs me in all this excitement and asks something like, "What about what Steve Spurrier said about your schedule? "

That's where watching my father's responses to big wins and big losses came in. The first thing that popped into my mind was something you would have said, Dad: "Well, he was probably right. I guess we have been playing a weak schedule."

They pick that up on all the highlight shows. And I look like the gracious winner with a sense of humor.

At the end of that same season, we lost to Alabama. And on our last series of the game, we miss on fourth and 3 by just a skin. And the fans want me to blame the officials' measurement.

I say, "No, it's not their fault." And I get credit again for not whining.

The thing is, the stories in the papers aren't written until after those postgame interviews. And the TV guys have to get their coaches' sound bites. What you say is going to be the final paragraph or two in tomorrow's game story and tonight's sports highlight. It's your last chance to influence the outcome of the game.

You're trying to say something that shows they didn't beat you down, you didn't lose your head, you're not going to blame other people. You don't win by going out there and throwing your chair, blaming the officials, saying they played dirty, saying they shouldn't have won because yours is the better team. If you do that, you've just lost again.

It's one more example of what we mean when we say, "Winning's only part of the game." Everything is part of the game, part of the series of games, part of the career you're trying to build.

BOBBY: I do a lot of what you say without even thinking about it. But that's the first time I've heard it put exactly that way.

Of course, you're right. For me, though, a lot of that talking and joking after a game is for my own therapy. I need to get the feeling of failure out of my system. I need to get back in the flow of life going on regardless of the score of a dadgum football game. That's part of the ritual I need to get me ready to play again.

TERRY: I talk a pretty good game of coping with losing, don't I? A lot of that is a sermon I give myself. The trouble is, I'm not always in the pew listening. I'm worrying too much.

I think I especially needed to remember those lessons in '95, when I don't think I handled losing as well as I could have. There's a world of difference between the theory of handling losses and the fact of standing in front of a crowd of reporters who want to know why you blew it.

15

THE PUBLIC ARENA

BOBBY: I get a lot of credit for being open with the press, for being willing to talk about just about anything with visiting reporters. It was something I think I figured out pretty early, back when I was desperate for recognition at those little schools. You just cannot build a winning program without help from the media.

But that doesn't mean it doesn't hurt to be hanging out there in public all the time. You boys are going to find out that pretty quickly, if you haven't already. Lose a game here and there, especially a big game you're expected to win, and folks will turn on you in a second.

TERRY: You're right, it didn't take long. In '95, after all I'd learned about not snapping back at reporters, I got defensive when the pressure built after losses to LSU, Arkansas, and Florida.

It was just so frustrating to me. I was trying to build such a positive attitude at Auburn, an attitude that could get us through occasional losses and into a long winning habit. And some of these guys in the media seemed intent on dividing the fans.

In '93 and '94, I could do no wrong. In '95, it was, "Well, the magic is finally gone . . . Wonder Boy ain't so wonderful anymore."

I haven't been around this long enough to roll with the punches the way you do, Dad.

BOBBY: Heck, I'm still learning my lessons, too. Just when I think I have the whole process figured out, along comes something that throws me for a loop.

TERRY: The problem is, people live vicariously through these football programs to the extent that their pride is shattered when you lose. If you're on TV and lose, they see that as tarnishing the image of the school in front of the whole nation.

It's like there are two completely different games going on at the same time. There's the one you're direct-ing on the field with real players, with a game plan of real plays, real assignments, and real responsibilities. Then there's the game in fans' minds.

For them, it's almost like a fairy-tale contest, with good guys and bad guys and the hero always winning because he has the purest heart. Of course, everybody believes their team, their school, has the purest heart. So they deserve to always win. Auburn is always supposed to get the girl.

If Auburn doesn't win, it's because the coach or the

players or both did something to interfere with Auburn's destiny. You betrayed the school.

BOBBY: I get letters all the time: "Dear Coach, we're so sorry our boys laid down like they did against so-and-so. I know they disappointed you the way they disappointed us. I sure hope they play like Florida State players next week."

Now those folks think they're being sympathetic with me, that we could have won if only our boys had tried harder. They refuse to give any credit to the other team. They don't think opponents have anything to do with football. It's amazing.

TERRY: As a coach, you try not to be responsible for the game going on in fans' imaginations. You've got enough to handle with the one on the field. But you can't help it. The fans' game is what fills the stadiums and brings the TV cameras. It's the only game that reporters know to talk and write about. And the truth is, it's the game that builds programs that attract coaches like us.

We all want to play at the top. But the closer you get to the top the more crowded the arena is with fan expectations and anxiety. Win and they'll give you anything; lose and they'll take it all away.

BOBBY: Well, if you think losing a game or two brings out the critics, try having a losing season. I have lost more games than I've won only twice in my career. One was the very first year at Florida State, where I took over a group that had gone 0–11, 1–10, and 3–8 under two different coaches in the three previous years. When we went 5–6 in '76, the fans were ready to elect me governor.

The only other time I had a losing year was in '74 at West Virginia. We were hit hard with injuries and couldn't buy a break. We finished 4–7, and it was like I had disgraced the whole state.

TOMMY: If it hadn't been for that year, Dad, I think Terry, Jeff, and I would have gone into this business with totally unrealistic expectations. You won so much the example could have been deceiving. But in '74 we all got a pretty good taste of what it could be like.

I was on the team that year, and I remember walking across campus and seeing sheets hanging out of the dorm windows: "Bowden's Got to Go!" They had a dummy dressed like you hanging in effigy from a big tree in the middle of campus.

There was an editorial in the student newspaper. "Why don't we fire Bowden? Let's get rid of him." And they said something in there about the head coach not even having the respect of his players.

I cut that editorial out and stuck it in my wallet. What I was going to do with that, I didn't know. But about six months later I was at a hot dog place frequented by students from the university, and I pulled out the editorial and showed it to a girl I knew.

"Have you ever heard of the guy who wrote this?"

She told me he was the president of a fraternity on campus. So I called the fraternity house and asked for the guy. "Are you going to be in tonight?"

"Yeah," he said.

So I got some of my buddies on the football team to go with me over to that fraternity house. They're big guys, maybe five or six of them, six-six, 270 pounds. We knock on the door. They let us in. The guy we're looking for is in the basement, they say. So down the stairs I go with all these guys following me.

We're attracting plenty of attention. But these frat guys are my size. They aren't going to do anything to challenge these huge players.

I walk up to the president and pull out the editorial. "Did you write this?"

Yes, he admits he had.

"Well, that's my father. You said the players don't respect Bowden. Here are some players. Why don't you ask them if they respect him?"

By this time, I think he was willing to do just about anything we asked. So I say, "What you wrote wasn't true. I want a retraction."

And we got one.

BOBBY: I have to admit getting a kick out of hearing that story years later. But it would have gotten us all in trouble if it had come out at the time. I hope the lesson you took away from that wasn't about how to handle the media when they say something you don't like.

TOMMY: No, it was about what you can expect if you make a living in this profession. It's about how quickly people turn around on you.

It's something you've got to learn if you're going to be a coach, especially in a high-profile program. And I learned it—secondhand from you, to begin with, then firsthand when I got to Auburn and had those two tough years before Terry came.

Coach Dye was the head coach, but I was running the offense. I had to answer the questions from reporters when we were losing half our games.

"You said this team was improving. What happened?"

And I would sit there and try to explain, all the time knowing that whatever I said could be construed as criticism of a player, and he would read it the next day in the paper or see it on TV. So I had to walk the line of being as honest as I could, while offering no excuses and saying nothing that would damage team morale. But if you're not winning, those kinds of answers aren't the ones that reporters want to hear.

Fortunately, I had the model of you, Dad. You're the master of not responding to negative criticism. I just kept thinking: "If you can't stand the heat . . ."

BOBBY: I had begun to think I was an expert on handling the heat until '94, when we got hit with that Foot Locker business. That opened up a whole new dimension.

Somebody from Las Vegas that I've never heard of in my life comes to Tallahassee because we're on our way to becoming national champions and because so many of our players have hopes of playing in the NFL. These guys are agents—or represent agents—who buy our kids clothes and shoes and give them some spending money with the idea of signing them up. It's all against NCAA rules, of course, but we don't know a thing about it until *Sports Illustrated* puts us on the cover.

It was like a dam broke. Reporters, investigators, lawyers were everywhere. All those years of trying to do things the right way didn't seem to count for anything. In the public's mind, we were accused, so we were guilty. FSU stood for Free Shoes University.

I tell you, though, I sure am glad we had spent all those years keeping our noses clean. Because if we hadn't, every single thing we'd ever done wrong would have come out in the investigation. My career would have been ruined. If I had known about these agents and had been covering it up, if I had been helping them, I would have had to resign.

In terms of public relations, that's the worst year I've ever had. When the story broke, I was out on our usual booster club tour, playing in local golf tournaments and speaking at banquets. Everywhere I turned, somebody was jumping out behind a bush to interrogate me.

A guy hid in a stairwell in Sarasota to get to me. Then, we go down to Clewiston, Florida, where a helicopter lands on the ninth hole, and this TV crew gets out demanding an interview right there. In Atlanta, another station tried the same thing.

For the first time in my career, I shut up like a clam. I didn't talk to nobody. I told the athletic department that I didn't even want to talk to my mama. I just got tired of it. It's all anybody wanted to talk about, and behind every question was this assumption that I knew all about these agents coming in here and didn't lift a finger.

After all those years, I thought I had insulated myself pretty well against the things people can say about you. But this hurt. I just couldn't believe people thought I would lie. And it's taken me this long to get over it.

TOMMY: That kind of experience can force you into a shell if you're not careful. In a way, I guess, it's a good thing that you can't run and hide somewhere when the media pressure hits. You're forced to deal with it in the open. This is a very public business and you don't have a choice about going on TV or talking to newspaper people.

TERRY: And, as our father taught us, it helps to have a sense of humor. Tommy may have become a better student of that than me.

After the Arkansas loss in '95, I had to leave to visit a friend in West Virginia whose mother was sick. Tommy, as offensive coordinator, and Wayne Hall, who was then our defensive coordinator, sat in for me at the weekly press conference.

Of course, after a loss like that, when you meet with the media there's this critical tone in the air. And Wayne, being as experienced as he is, tried to defuse it a little by reminding reporters a defeat like that hurts the coaches and players as much as the fans. He told them about a little old lady who put him on the spot after the game.

This lady, says Wayne, "comes up to me and says, 'Coach Hall, I told you this was going to happen. I told you you weren't going to take this game seriously enough and you would come in here and lose this game.' "

It hurt his feelings, said Wayne, "that she thought I

didn't care enough, that our players hadn't prepared enough."

Well, pretty soon it was time for Tommy, who was sitting right next to Wayne. "Well," said Tommy, "the first thing I want to do, Coach Hall, is apologize for my mother coming up and saying that to you."

16

LEADERSHIP AND LOYALTY

TERRY: I tell you one thing you absolutely must have if you are to be successful in the public arena: loyalty. I think it's the most important trait in coaching.

In Alabama, just about everyone thinks that what we do on Saturday afternoons in the fall is the most important thing happening in the state. When Auburn plays Alabama, those three and a half hours are the most important three and a half hours of the year. Everyone is affected. If you lose, there are thousands of people who feel as if their hearts have been ripped out.

If you coach in that environment, you had better make sure that there is a safe place you can go, that there is a small group of loyal people you can turn to who don't doubt you can overcome that loss and win again. You must create that atmosphere with your staff.

And you must maintain it, even if your support starts to crumble elsewhere.

My people have to believe, "Terry knows how to win. If it gets shaky around here, just hang in there. Because he can do it."

I don't think I've ever demanded more loyalty from a staff than I demanded during the '95 season. I got a sense of what you must have gone through in '91 and '92, Tommy. And because you went through that and came out the other side, you could help me when things got tough in '95.

After we lost at Louisiana State in the third game of the season and I became convinced we had to change our offense, I put enormous pressure on our offensive coaches. I know I drove them crazy coming in every day with new plays and new ideas, demanding that they make the kinds of wholesale changes that you usually make in the spring. But they hung with me.

TOMMY: And we ended up setting twenty-something records with an offense we completely revamped in the middle of the year.

We were all over the board. We ran the gamut philosophically. We were meeting through lunch. We were meeting at night. You knew I was going to be there. I'm your brother. But you were confident that the others felt the same way. If you said, "Do it," you knew we would find a way to get it done. I don't think you would have tried that with very many staffs.

TERRY: It would have been even riskier without you there. Remember that plane trip back from Baton Rouge?

You sat next to me while I was rattling on about all the changes we had to make. And you said, "You're right. That's the direction we have to go. Go ahead with it."

Coming from you, that meant a lot more to me than it would have if I'd heard it from somebody else. Lord knows, the last thing on your mind is saying something just to please me. You'll tell me what you're thinking. And in this case, what I was considering was exactly what you had been advocating since I came to Auburn—more of the no-huddle, four-wide-receiver offense.

But I needed to hear that confirmation from you. In those first couple hours after a loss, doubt creeps in: "Have I lost the magic?"

TOMMY: It's the same with all of us. That's what you feel at first. And if you need some help with self-doubt it comes from all those people who are analyzing and overanalyzing every move we make in football in this state.

By the time we played LSU, I had been coaching for nineteen years, and I had been through some tough times. When you face those times and work your way through them, it gives you confidence you can do it again. But I don't think I took any loss harder than that one at LSU. It was only the second time we'd been beaten in the time you'd been at Auburn. And it was the first time we had lost, then had to get the team up for the next game. When we lost to Alabama, it came at the end of the '94 season. So a lot depended on us coming up with a plan the players believed in.

TERRY: And the staff *had* to believe in order to convince the players.

Out among the fans there is always that suspicion that, "Well, maybe he was lucky those first two years. Maybe things just went his way. Now, his luck has changed."

There will be pressures on assistant coaches to point fingers somewhere else: "It wasn't me; it was the offensive line coach's fault." Or, "How can we win if the defense can't hold anybody?"

That's how doubts spread. They create cracks that split wide open and divide staffs. And no one can win with a divided staff.

I know you won't talk about those first two years at Auburn, Tommy. You don't want anything to sound like an excuse. But there's no doubt that's the kind of danger that staff was in with an NCAA investigation going on, a head coach on his way out, and the losses piling up.

TOMMY: But this group stayed together, Terry.

Where I helped, I think, was during that period when we were jumping around from offense to offense. I could come into your office and say, "This is what the guys are concerned about . . . These are some of the things you can do to reassure them . . . These are the things I can smooth over with them."

We could all stay on the same page. But none of that would have been possible without complete loyalty.

BOBBY: Well, you boys have hit on something crucial here. Crucial and complicated. When I first came to Florida State in '76 and was going through the things I expected out of our staff, the word I said over and over again was *loyalty*.

"Men," I said, "without loyalty, we can't have anything. If I hear of any of you talking about me downtown or questioning anything I do, I'll consider that disloyal."

It's absolutely essential to leading a program at this level. You might be able to run other businesses by consensus. You might be able to take votes on what's acceptable and not acceptable. But coaching ain't a democracy. Nobody needs to put a sign on my desk that says, "The buck stops here." Because that's just assumed. I'm held responsible for everything. And if I'm responsible, I need to have authority, and I need to believe that everyone on my staff accepts that authority without question.

When you compete in public week in and week out, a sense of urgency is imposed on you that just isn't there in most professions. You don't have to wait for the annual report to know how you're doing. Just look up at the scoreboard. You can bet everybody else is. If you miss it, tune in to the news that night, because they'll replay it so everybody knows how you stand.

In that environment, you had better demand—and get—loyalty from your people. But here's where it gets complicated. Don't you also owe loyalty in return?

I always had a deep sense of loyalty all my life. If I'm working for Howard College, I'm gonna give it all I got for Howard. I'm not interested in anything else. If I'm at Florida State, I'm gonna be loyal to Florida State. At West Virginia, I was about ready to pledge those people that I would be there the rest of my life. And then came that '74 season where I went 4–7.

All of a sudden, they quit inviting me to their house. All of a sudden they quit inviting me to their get-togethers. Now, I don't care about going to all that stuff anyway. But I like to know they wanted me there.

You hear people talking and read editorials and start thinking: "Hold it now, I'm thinking about staying here the rest of my life and being loyal. And look what they're doing to me because I'm losing a few games. I'm having a bad year. I've got both my quarterbacks in the hospital, and they're going to fire me if I can't score."

That year, our last ball game was against Virginia Tech in Blacksburg, Virginia. They were favored. And if they won, we'd finish with a 3–8 record. I was catching heck throughout the state. I had heard that at several of those games there were meetings of big boosters to get rid of Coach Bowden. They already had somebody they wanted to bring in.

So we're about to play that last ball game, and the night before, the team doctors—three who traveled with us every trip and were very well-connected—come by my room. "We just want you to know that we're behind you all the way," they say. "We also want you to know that the athletic council met, and they're behind you."

I didn't know what they were talking about. Anyway, we play the next day and win in a major upset. The president and the athletic director kept saying they were behind me. But there were a lot of people stirring out there, guys who were former presidents of the booster board. Some of them were trying to undermine things and get another coach ready to come in as soon as they could get me fired.

TERRY: That year taught us a few things, too, Dad. We've already talked about our education in the fickleness of fans. But '74 provided a pretty good lesson in the politics of big-time college football, too. Loyalty from boosters and university officials is always conditional on your success.

What's amazing is how, after tasting a little of that, you didn't become cynical about the whole notion of loyalty to institutions that hire and fire you based on wins and losses.

BOBBY: Well, you've got to remember that if that had never happened at West Virginia, I probably would never have ended up at Florida State. I would have stayed right there.

Of course, I know that the same thing could happen in Tallahassee, even after all the success we've had. All I needed was to drop three or four games in a season the last few years and the talk would have started: "Ol' Bobby is getting senile, now. Better put him out to pasture."

But the truth is, I probably talk a better game of cynicism than I play. Since I've been at Florida State, I've been offered so many jobs, it's pitiful. It started back in '79 and '80. My second year here, we won ten ball games and went to a bowl.

We were nationally ranked, which we hadn't been in years. My third year, we were undefeated, then lost in a bowl. I was hot. I was getting calls from the pros and other colleges. But nothing looked so attractive to me that I would have considered breaking a contract. The closest I came to it was in '86. And that's a good example of how torn up you can get over the loyalty issue.

We were set to play in the All-American Bowl in Birmingham when Ray Perkins resigned at Alabama. My name came popping up as a candidate for the coaching job. And I kept running into all these people, including the governor of the state, who are asking me, "You're coming back to Alabama, aren't you? You're coming back?"

I'm thinking, "They're fixing to offer me the job." I heard the president of the university wanted to talk to me. And I made it clear that I didn't want to talk to him unless he was going to offer me the job. I wasn't going to go in there and try out for it.

I'm asking the big boosters I know, "You think he's going to offer me the job?" And I'm hearing back, "Oh yeah, you're his choice."

Well, that turned out not to be true. When I finally did get to see the president, it was during a formal interview in a room before the whole dadgum committee. Which embarrassed me, because I hadn't told anyone at Florida State that I was interviewing for anything. I never would have walked into that room if I had known that was what they were going to do.

But the day before the bowl game I didn't know any of that. I was thinking I stood a pretty good chance of being offered the Alabama job and that, if I was being totally honest with myself, I stood a pretty good chance of taking it. This was my home state and the job I had always dreamed of having. It seemed like it was meant to happen.

So while I'm thinking all of this, we have this big Florida State pep rally at Five Points in Birmingham. The streets are all blocked off, and there are all these people just packed in there. The band's there with the cheerleaders, and I'm supposed to speak.

Ann and I drive down there with other people from the school. I have to stand on the back of this big flatbed truck, looking out over what must be thousands of people. The band is playing, and there's all this excitement. All these people are looking up there at me. And I'm saying to myself, "Bobby, here you are, fixin' to talk to your group. They're all excited about being in this bowl game. And you're probably going to be at Alabama next year."

I start to get tears in my eyes. The band is playing. I'm fired up for Florida State, talking about playing in that game. And all the time I'm thinking I might be the head coach at another school in a week.

It liked to kill me. Thank goodness, I didn't have to make that decision. But I mean to tell you, that was getting to me. It's not like all they had to do was offer it and I would have taken it. But I think I would have.

As I look back, I can see I wasn't what the president really wanted. He was looking for an Ivy League type of guy. And that ain't me. And that's not Alabama. Poor ol' Bill Curry got the job and did great. But they got rid of him. They got rid of the president, too. And I stayed at Florida State, where, in '87, we started that record string of ten-win seasons that made us one of the two or three teams to beat in all of college football. It turned out for the best for everybody.

TERRY: I think you do have to feel that sense of loyalty to the people who hired you and to the fans. It's just that you have to understand that the only way you can guarantee they'll stay with you is if you win.

When you lose a couple of games, fans and boosters are going to second-guess themselves and you. When you win again, they'll all come back. What you can't have is your own staff getting caught up in that ebb and flow of faith and enthusiasm. They have to be consistent. They have to believe in you, and they have to show it when others question your abilities.

A reporter or a booster will call an assistant coach and say, "Ol' so-and-so ain't doin' a very good job with his players, is he?" Well, it's not enough for my guy to just keep his mouth shut. That amounts to confirmation of that suspicion. And that's disloyal. We have got to create the safe place. We've got to have trust and faith in one another. Or we'll all go down together.

BOBBY: You know I've preached that all my career. But part of what I mean about loyalty going the other way is the loyalty you have to show to your own people.

The more success we've had at Florida State, the more brilliant young coaches I have calling and writing wanting jobs. Over twenty years, I could have replaced a lot of my coaches with the next offensive or defensive genius to come along. But I didn't do that. Now, I've had assistants quit to move on to what they thought were better jobs, but I never replaced one just because I thought a better guy was waiting in the wings.

Over the course of twenty-five years, I've told three or four men that I wanted them to leave. But it was always because I thought that if they stayed it would cause a morale problem. As long as they were doing the job I demanded, I never considered firing anybody. So, except for a few who've gone on to take jobs with more responsibility or money, I've held on to the same core of guys for a decade. That gives a team a sense of continuity and it builds the kind of loyalty I require.

TERRY: That's a good point, Dad. People ask why you don't grab this guy from over here, that guy from over there and build this super-staff of coaches who are each the best guy in the country at coaching his specialty. Well, I would rather mold a staff that feels comfortable with me and with each other than pull together a group of geniuses who are going to be rivals.

If they have weaknesses in a particular technique or style, it's my job to help them acquire the skills they need. It's my job to motivate them to become better coaches.

BOBBY: I've always felt that you don't want sameness on the staff. If everybody is a Vince Lombardi type, then you're going to have coaches running all over each other. If all of them are meek, then you're going to have a staff with no backbone. But if you have a mix of the go-getters and the quiet ones, they'll blend together. And you often end up with a whole that is greater than the sum of the parts.

TERRY: When a staff grows together in that way it's easier for them to see that their individual ambitions are all wrapped up in the success of the team. That's another way in which the pressures of our profession help clarify goals. In most businesses, especially ones with huge workforces, there can be all kinds of groups working to produce a product that's not immediately apparent to individual workers. You can have rivalries and resentments in those groups and still stay in business. Executives can be at war with one another and advance up the ladder.

But in our profession, where a staff of ten—a head coach and nine assistants—is held accountable for everything that happens in plain sight on Saturday afternoon, there's no mistaking the relationship between individual effort and team goals. Everyone wins and loses together. And the only way an individual advances is through the success of the team.

It's about the most clear-cut relationship between loyalty and leadership that I know about.

Every year, before the season begins, I remind my staff of this: "If it's your desire to be a head coach, the best way to get into that position is to help this team win. If you recruit and develop national championship caliber players, you contribute to this team's ultimate success. That success makes you more valuable and more attractive to schools seeking head coaches. It's the fastest route to where you want to go.

"I'll help you get there. I'll do everything I can to make you a better coach here. And I'll do everything I can to help you get that next job. You can be interested in any job you want but one—the one I have. You can't want my job and stay here, because I plan to be coaching at Auburn for the next twenty-five years. And if you're not committed to helping me do that, you're going to have to go."

17

LEADERSHIP AND CHANGE

BOBBY: After all this talk about the lessons you take away from coaching football, maybe we ought to focus on one that probably doesn't get as much attention as it should: dealing with the necessity of change. You win by adapting.

I know this is a big topic among business leaders. I hear all the time about the need to cope with change in marketplaces and the need to adapt to change within companies. This, evidently, is a period in American business when change is on everybody's mind. But it's not something you hear a lot from football coaches. We're more apt to stand up in front of audiences and talk about the values of determination and perseverance.

I guess that's because we're a fairly conservative lot. We're big on repetition. We practice the same thing over and over so that our players learn to react to situations instead of having to waste time thinking about them.

There's a certain way we want people to block, to wrap their arms when they tackle, to catch passes with their hands instead of their bodies. We coach quarterbacks on how many steps to take and receivers on how many yards to run before making their cuts. It must seem like football comes with a set of the most rigid rules imaginable. You have to do everything exactly the same way every time.

Well, that's true as far as it goes. Because football has so many people on the field at once, because it's so complicated strategically, the best way to cut down on confusion and build confidence is to put players in the most familiar situations you can. You want them to recognize where they belong in every play and do what you coached them to do every time.

But hey, life doesn't turn out to be all that predictable. And neither does football. When you face an inferior opponent, it's possible to impose your system on his, to overpower him with the stuff you want to do. But when you face someone with the same kind of talent you have or someone who's prepared themselves especially well, the winner of that contest is apt to be the guy who can adjust more quickly. It's adapt or die.

This is such an obvious requirement in football, I think we forget to mention it. But if there's one thing that connects all consistent winners in highly competitive situations, it's the ability to deal with change—to force unwelcome change on other people and to adapt quickly to the changes they force on you.

TERRY: Yeah, but there's danger, too, in jumping into change prematurely. You can let a situation rattle you so much you abandon a winning plan and throw everything into confusion. That's something I have to tell myself all the time.

From where you sit, Dad, after all your years of experience, you can probably spot the times when you have to hold 'em and the times you have to fold 'em. But it's tough. I know there's a graveyard full of ex-coaches who changed when they shouldn't have and another graveyard just as full with those who failed because they couldn't change in time. That's one of the things that keeps us up at night.

For me, two Louisiana State games—the one we won, barely, in '94 and the one we lost, barely, in '95—make perfect illustrations. In '94, our offense couldn't do a thing. It took four touchdowns by our defense to pull out a 30–26 win that left a bad taste in people's mouths. Everybody seemed to think the answer was to yank our quarterback and start somebody else. The fans certainly wanted that. And I think if we took a vote in our offensive meetings, it would have been just me and Tommy on the other side. But that's enough of a majority when you're the head coach.

I stuck with our quarterback, and he went on to lead us to a 9-1-1 season in '94 and help set all those offensive records in '95. Resisting change was the right decision at that moment.

Then came the '95 LSU game. Once again, it was the third game of the season, a time when you're still working out the personality of your team. And once again, we couldn't seem to get into the end zone. We had worked on a four-wide-receiver package a lot in practice, but I was reluctant to use it in a game that was so close.

We were down 12–6 late in the fourth quarter when time forced me to go to the shotgun. And we drove the ball right down the field and were throwing into the end zone when time ran out. I made the change too late in that one. If we had gone to the shotgun earlier, we probably would have won that game.

Change is hard because we fear the unknown. There's comfort in routine and repetition—especially when you win. By the time we got to the Alabama game in '94, we hadn't lost since I'd been at Auburn. But when we came back in '95 with the same offense, people had learned to adjust. They just weren't going to let us do the same thing. So we had to change.

JEFF: It took people two years to figure out how to deal with your offense, though. If you had changed earlier, you risked confusing a team you were just taking over.

Here's the way I look at it: I want to come up with things that have never been done before. I want to direct innovative offenses. I love the scheming part of this job. But I also believe the key to making adjustments in this profession—and maybe in life, too—is having simple standards to go by.

Keep it simple and let great athletes make great plays. When it's time to change, you can modify simple plans more quickly and easily than complicated ones.

TOMMY: When you came to Auburn in '93, Terry, we had the great athletes for that straightforward I formation offense. Ten of those twenty-two starters are going to play in the NFL. So putting those guys in that offense was the right thing to do.

I may have been advocating a transition to the shotgun offense, but it's hard to argue with 20-1-1 those first two years. And I don't think we had a bad game plan going into LSU. In fact, I probably would have moved a little more slowly to make the transition than you did, Terry.

BOBBY: Y'all are right. It's more complicated than I made it sound. Here's the thing you have to watch out about, especially after a loss.

I watch film on Sunday and Monday and spot all these ways we can attack the next opponent. I can sit down and draw up a new play for every situation that would just kill 'em. I'm saying to myself, "Boy, this play would hurt 'em. And this one and this one . . ."

The first thing you know, you've got thirty new plays. But you can't do all of them. There's no way you can teach your kids all those plays in the week you have to prepare. You might can develop one of them. You might get two. But the worst thing you can do is go and try to put all thirty of them in there. Then you won't be able to do anything. You can't get enough repetitions in the days you have to practice.

You've got to practice it against this defense, in case they do this, then another version in case they slip into that defense. You've got to work on it from the right hash mark, then the left, now from the middle of the field. What about the goal line?

There may be five variations of that one play. All of a sudden those thirty new plays become 150. There's no way you're going to have enough time.

Terry, you're like me. You see all these things and you get in there with your coaches offering all these new plays. But you've got to realize at some point that everything you want is not possible. I go into my staff and say, "Boy, this looks good. And this, and this." But I also tell them I don't expect them to do every little thing I seem interested in. They'll know when something's really important to me. The rest they can pick and choose.

"I know y'all can't do all this," I say. "Just concentrate on the few things you think will work, and let's get them right."

If you don't do that, you can drive your staff crazy.

TERRY: I know I did some of that in '95. My problem is that if I see something I want to do, I want it done right now.

That's where Tommy came in in '95. I was insisting we make all these changes immediately. And the staff was trying. But I needed Tommy to put the brakes on me a little bit and to be a buffer between me and some of the other offensive coaches.

TOMMY: It was a reversal of roles in a lot of ways. Here Terry was putting in the offense that I had been urging on him for years. And I was trying to slow him down so we could make the transition without busting our gears. And we managed to do it.

TERRY: Then came the problem of fans' resistance to change. A lot of them are worried we're getting too far away from that I formation offense. They're afraid we're "sissifying" Southern football with a "finesse" game. Boy, they hate that. "Auburn won with Bo Jackson and all those other great tailbacks running the ball. Now you Bowdens want to pass the dang ball all over the place!"

They're not noticing, I guess, that we still have running backs gaining 1,000 yards a season. All they see is that shotgun and a bunch of receivers. For them, the best argument against change is that 20-1-1 record.

BOBBY: It's hard to see the need for change when you're doing well. Changes are always easier to make when things can't get much worse.

When I hit Tallahassee in '76, I brought all kinds of change. People were desperate for it, since in the three years before I got there the Seminoles had won a total of four games. They were begging for something new.

Against Oklahoma in the third game of that first season, I benched a bunch of older guys and started seven freshmen. We lost, but it sent a signal. New coach, new ways of doing things. I got a lot of credit for making a change like that. But it was a low-risk move, given the place we were starting from.

Now, go forward fifteen years. That '76 season is ancient history. In fact, we haven't had a losing season since then. In '92, I had a program that had put up ten or more wins for five years in a row. Every year we were within striking distance of a national championship. Now, you come to the point where change carries enormous risk.

For a couple of years, you had been touting your shotgun ideas, Tommy, and I was interested but just too dadgum scared to mess with what was clearly working for us. We put some of that offense in and tried it out during spring practices. But I was too nervous to go to it regularly.

Then, in '92, Charlie Ward's first year at quarterback, we're losing big at Georgia Tech and go to the no-huddle shotgun to catch up, and the darn thing is absolutely unstoppable. Unstoppable. So that becomes our offense.

The funny thing is, that offense is in itself an adjustment forced by the rising dominance of defenses. Defensive coaches found a way to get at least one more man than you could block up on the line. That wads up the running lanes and frees a guy to rush the passer in the I formation. Going to four wideouts and getting your quarterback in the shotgun away from the line of scrimmage was a way to cause problems for that defense.

So instead of us imposing our offensive will on defenses, this whole no-huddle shotgun was just a way to adapt to a change in the game.

JEFF: For a while it looked as if offenses were moving ahead of defenses. Steve Spurrier at Florida; us at Florida State; Terry and Tommy at Auburn; and some other schools with the right match of talent have gone to these high-scoring offenses. But it was going to be just a matter of time before somebody on the other side of the ball came up with their adjustments.

We saw that at Virginia, where in '95 we lost our first Atlantic Coast Conference game. That game was a credit to the Virginia coaches' preparations. They came at us with something we had seen but had not practiced against very much. It was a kind of prevent defense, rushing three men and dropping eight back in coverage. We knew how to attack it, but we just weren't prepared to go out there for a whole game and do it.

The way it really hurt us is that it shook our confidence. Our receivers were used to getting open. Our quarterback was used to seeing someone to throw to. Suddenly, the margin of error was cut way down. There were still holes in the defense, but they were much narrower. And that got to us. We couldn't do the kinds of things that would have allowed us to adjust. We didn't execute. We didn't adapt quickly enough. And we lost.

We were in that offense for three years, and people finally realized what they had to do. Now, we'll see a version of that defense every Saturday until we come up with some answers and make the adjustments.

BOBBY: Here's something else that affects your adjustment. And it's not so obvious to fans. You can trick yourself into thinking that a fast, high-scoring offense will give you a cushion against playing weak defense yourself. To a certain extent that's true—as long as the other guys let you keep scoring at will. But the thing that happens when your own defense gives up lots of points is you start worrying that you must score and you must score fast to keep the edge.

That's going to tempt you into passing on every down and maybe throwing downfield into dangerous coverage. You narrow your own options, which means you're working right into the defense's hands.

What makes any offensive strategy work is keeping options open. The defense has to believe you can run the ball a couple of different ways and you can pass it a half dozen ways. They can't load up to stop just one or two kinds of plays. But if you throw out everything but the big, quick-hit plays, you make things much less complicated for the other guys. And suddenly every receiver is double- and triple-covered.

When we played Notre Dame in '94, they concentrated on stopping our shotgun and darn near shut us down. Then we started running the ball, which seems like the absolute last thing you'd want to do against a team that sees all those Big 10 running teams. But they had spent so much time working on our passing game, they couldn't contain the run. We adjusted; they didn't. We ended up with 377 rushing yards against them and won the game.

Against Virginia, we might have been able to do the same thing. But we gave up 27 points in the first half—something we haven't done in eight or nine years. And I'm figuring if they got 27 in the first half, they can get 27 more in the second. That's 54 points. So we're going to need a bunch of points in a hurry. We can't afford to be running the ball 3, 4, 5 yards a carry. It takes fifty seconds for a running play, only three seconds for an incomplete pass.

Now, if somebody had told me our defense was going to hold them to only 6 points in the second half, I would have gone more to the run. And there's a good chance we could have pulled it out. As it was, we ended up less than a foot shy of scoring the winning touchdown.

That's what happens when you're winning, when you're No. 1 in the polls and go into a game with what should be superior talent. Change is not something you're thinking about. "Hey," you say, "we've been winning doing this one thing. Let's don't do anything to mess it up."

Those kinds of situations are still teaching me lessons about the need to adapt. It's a permanent process. When I stop learning and adjusting, nobody will have to tell me to retire. There ain't much wiggle room at our level. When we stop adapting, we'll be losing so much that I'll want out.

TERRY: The trick is in making the changes just before you're forced to. To win consistently, you have to be just a little ahead of the wave.

One thing we all do is scout ourselves. We assign somebody to watch our games or analyze our film to reveal our tendencies. When we line up in this formation, do we always run to the right? If we put this receiver on this side of the ball, is that a key that we're throwing his way? Even without knowing it, we fall into comfortable patterns. When we become that predictable, we have to change.

BOBBY: That goes for my famous trick plays, too. The whole idea behind a trick play is surprise. But I've done my favorite reverses and halfback passes so many times in certain situations that coaches have picked up on it. When I look at film after games, I see defenses line up in ways that would be the stupidest possible alignments—if they didn't know I was calling one of my favorites.

Of course, I've outsmarted myself the other way, too. I'll call a certain play that picks up 10 yards. I call it again, and it gets 12. I call it again, and the same darn play gets another 10.

"Now," I'll say to myself, "there ain't no way I'm calling that again, because they must know by now what's coming." So the next time we're in the same situation, I call the same formation but something that goes in the opposite direction. And the dadgum thing runs right into their coverage. If I had called that same play one more time, I would have caught them in the wrong alignment again and gotten another big gain.

Sometimes, if you're not careful, you end up playing yourself.

Here's what all this boils down to. Coaching, managing people, planning strategies—they're full of necessary contradictions. You've got to outprepare the other guy, plan for every contingency, and practice your plan until it comes naturally.

Then you've got to be willing to throw the whole thing out and wing it.

When we go into a ball game, my offensive coaches and I have developed a game plan. We have it all written down: Here's what to do when it's second down and long. Here's our favorite play for third and short, for fourth and goal to win the game. Here's what we'll do when we're backed up close to our own end zone. Here's what we like for first down in their territory.

If we get into a game and all that stuff works, fine. But if we go three downs and punt, three downs and punt for a few series, 70 percent of the time that game plan goes out the window.

Experiencing success gives you the courage to do that. But there's a catch. And remember, this is coming from a guy who fears losing more than anything in the world: If you ain't willing to take the risk, you ain't gonna win enough to get the experience.

Because you boys were able to get a little secondhand experience watching me, maybe that gave you a leg up in the profession that's become our family business. When I watch each of you now, I see all the combinations of Ann and I and the influences you've had on one another. I see how you picked up this idea or that one, how you've become your own kinds of coaches by taking what you need from me and from one another. You've all adapted in your own ways. And you've all been winners.

As a father, I probably wanted to insulate you from the pressure of having so many people, people you don't even know, depending on you to win a football game. But if I had done that, I would have insulated you from the experience you needed to do what makes you happiest.

It's all turned out for the best, hasn't it? I'm at the stage of my life where my own career is safe. But there's not a dadgum thing I can do about protecting y'all from the ups and downs of this game. There probably never was.

I've preached till I'm blue in the face that anybody who can't stand the heat ought to get out of the kitchen. You've heard it a million times. Since y'all have come running toward the stove as fast as you can, I reckon you're as prepared as you're going to get for whatever comes. So I've made up my mind to try to quit worrying and to start enjoying.

AFTERWORD

As this book goes to press, the Bowdens are preparing for another season of high pressure and high expectations.

Bobby signed a new contract with Florida State that extends his tenure through the year 2000. His Seminoles beat Notre Dame 31–26 in the Orange Bowl on January 1, 1996, and attracted a recruiting class that once again ranks among the best in the nation.

The bowl victory extends Bobby Bowden's record streak to eleven consecutive post-season wins and reaffirms Florida State's status as the winningest college football program of the '90s. The tradition is expected to continue. Before spring practice, Danny Sheridan, sports analyst for CNN and *USA Today*, predicted the Seminoles would enter the 1996 season picked No. 1 or No. 2 in the country.

Auburn, making its first appearance in a bowl game since 1990, showed its post-season inexperience against a veteran Penn State squad in the January 1, 1996 Outback Bowl. The Tigers lost 43–14 in a Tampa monsoon. But a strong recruiting class and returning veterans at key positions make it likely Auburn will contend for this season's conference title and have another shot at a major bowl.

After the bowl, Terry Bowden replaced three assistants left from the Pat Dye era at Auburn, including defensive coordinator Wayne Hall. He hired the much-admired Alabama defensive coordinator Bill "Brother" Oliver to take over the defense and coach the secondary. That created a stir in a state divided by fierce allegiances to the two major football powers. And it bumped Terry's brother-in-law Jack Hines to coach inside linebackers.

The consensus in the family and on the coaching staff is that the moves are an important step in Terry's plan to build a loyal staff capable of attracting top talent and of dominating on both sides of the football. But the bowl loss and the staff turnover are certain to keep the off-season spotlight on the continuing adventures of the boy wonder coach and his family.

As always, said Robyn Hines, "All you have to do is win. That shuts everybody up."

To add to the excitement, on March 6, Terry's wife, Shyrl, gave birth to a baby girl, Jamie Taylor Bowden.

Tommy, given much of the credit for Auburn's high-potent mix of passing and running, was mentioned as a candidate for several vacant head coaching spots at the end of 1995. But the perfect job hasn't materialized. "I feel real comfortable right now just waiting for the right opportunity," he said.

As for the other Bowdens, Ann is in her usual spring routine of overseeing a charity cruise for the Baptist Children's Home and preparing for the annual city-a-day booster club tour with Bobby in April.

Steve decided to leave the higher education world, at least for the time being, to try his hand at real estate development. Jeff is looking forward to unleashing a group of wide receivers at Florida State likely to be rated among the best in all of college football in '96. And after the birth of her third son in September, Ginger has returned happily to her work as a prosecutor in Fort Walton Beach.